SIMPLE ABSENCE

SIMPLE ABSENCE

Poems and Reflections by

Nancy Fitz-Hugh Meneely

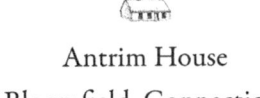

Antrim House
Bloomfield, Connecticut

Library of Congress Control Number: 2019942858

ISBN: 978-1-943826-58-2

First Edition, 2020

Printed & bound by Ingram Content Group

Book design by Rennie McQuilkin

Front cover art: oil on linen by Scott Kahn,
"Griswold Point December"

Antrim House
860.217.0023
AntrimHouseBooks@gmail.com
www.AntrimHouseBooks.com
400 Seabury Dr., #5196, Bloomfield, CT 06002

To family in all its dispositions, the fundamental cell in the body of the world.

More especially, to families who have lost each other one way or another and whom we hope to help to find the way back home.

Most especially, to Lilly and her family, who offer daily proof of the joys of life with two mothers.

ACKNOWLEDGMENTS

Thanks to the editors who previously published poems and prose in this book as follows:

"Milestones in the Mouth" published as "When a Girl Goes from Braces to Straight Teeth" in *The Washington Post Style Section,* October 1, 1998

"If I Wanted, Now I Could Give Myself" in the 2001 Awards Issue of *The Comstock Review*, judge Mary Oliver

"Palpation" in *The Annals of Internal Medicine,* April, 2002

"Reading Signs" in *Innisfree Poetry Journal,* September 2009

"Getting Glide" and "In the Long Afternoon of My Life" in the *Guilford Poets Guild 2009 Tenth Anniversary Anthology,* judge Gray Jacobik

"Sunday in Park with George" selected for performance by the East Haddam Stage Company in the November 2010 production of their Plays and Poetry series and again in their 2011 Audience Favorites production

"Sunday in Park with George in *Freshwater,* Spring 2014

"Not Spring Again" and "The World Going" in the *Guilford Poets Guild 2019 Tenth Anniversary Anthology*

"Sinkholes" in *Cider Press Review,* 2016

First, I honor my editor, publisher and beloved friend, Rennie McQuilkin, for his certainty, his ever-inspirational joy in life and the cherishing consideration he makes of even the very least of poems. I honor the motley groups that encourage (in its most particular meaning) the effort to keep the pen mightier than the sword and to steady movement for the good. In particular, I thank the members of Together We Rise, many of them poets, who counsel action and word with deep respect for both. I treasure the groups of writers who learn each other over the years and come to every meeting with ready honest comment and ready love. I would not want to do without The Connecticut River Poets, the Guilford Poets Guild, and the geographically scattered poets who gather once a year in Chester for a week of work and laughter. There's no way I could measure the thanks I owe them all or the awe in which I hold them. Special thanks to members of "The Salon", Julie and Charles, Gray and Bruce, Rennie and Sarah, and Gary, for the evenings which deepen love for the arts poetic, visual, and culinary, and each other.

I offer the special kind of thanks earned by cherished first readers Gray Jacobik, Jane Ulrich, and Anne Harding Woodworth.

I thank my family with all my heart: Gary, my husband, the world's most supportive man, whose steady insistence has carried this project from beginning to end; my daughter, Delia, and her wife, Sairy, and their astonishing child, Lilly, who nourish every day; Sarah and Dorothea, who inspire with love unique to siblings and by pursuing their own arts, musical and naturopathic.

Oddly, I offer an atheist's thanks to The First Congregational Church of Old Lyme for making warm room in its community and choir stall for a regretful unbeliever who, however, has fervent faith in the church community itself. It is easy to be a poet in a church that finds a place for a poem in every service.

TABLE OF CONTENTS

III. WEATHERING

IV. LITTLE DELIA

V. RECORDINGS

VI. THE WORLD COMING, THE WORLD GOING

VII. THE WHITE-HAIRED WOMAN

Alchemy at the River's Mouth

after Scott Kahn's "Griswold Point December"

Half-baffled in a ferment
of the stippling clouds,
the blue-edged sun
sends silver light

to plate a pathway
toward the fragile spit
that thwarts incursion
of the scrolling Sound.

Inside its safeguard,
shore accepts no more
than thumb and fingers
of the moon-drawn tide,

cutwork inlets cradled in alluvia,
infused with gold the shallows take
from what there is of warmth
in winter's sky.

SIMPLE ABSENCE

I. STILL LIVES

Still Life With Grandmother

Drugged with southern evening,
we fight the need to go to bed,
squabble over Hearts until
the youngest cousins cry.
Enough, enough, she scolds,
and sends us up the stairs.
We turn at the landing
to see if she will come
but she has bent to her nightwork
under the lamp, remote inside
the wingback chair.
Her shadowed face is stern.
We leave her to the stillness
she inhabits at night
since Grandfather sickened and died.

The peacock has descended
from the ridgepole.
Furled and unremarkable,
he drowses near the coop
where chickens fret
and mumble in their sleep.
Smells of boxwood, honeysuckle,
last year's leaves becoming dirt
sieve in through window screens
and dark contracts around the house.
She sits in her circle of light,
crochet needle flashing
in her tumbler hands,
growing one more bedspread.
She'll cover us all before she goes.

Upstairs, we're sleeping
greedily, storing ourselves
for another August day.
But she is only a passenger
in these hours, carried
with neither joy nor regret
toward the shortened rest of the old
and summer's long evaporation into fall.

A Shell Gas Attack

from the journal of Captain John K. Meneely, Sr.
France, 1918

The shells are dropping all around
The world is swallowed up in sound
The air is foul with lurking death
With gas, which drowns your very breath.

The big shells send their splinters great
Each sending out its ordained fate
The small 4.2s come crashing in
The rifles add their tiny din.

It's night, but just 'cause clocks say so
The sky is filled with reddened glow
The star shells burst to float on high
The rockets soar up in the sky.

The bursts of all these shells so near
Do they breed in us any fear?
No, not the shells, it's gas that starts
That cold gray chill into our hearts.

It comes so soft, you hear a thud
You almost think it's but a "dud"
But then you hear its soft burst too
And know it's gas, tonight, for you.

You see the sickish green cloud rise
But not like clouds, up toward the skies

No-No—it reaches out green hands
And round your man throws deadly bands.

It's "GAS" the cry goes up from all
It chills your heart like danger's call
It's "CEASE ALL WORK—STAND FAST YOU THERE
DON'T STIR UP CURRENTS IN THE AIR."

"WALK UP THE WIND, GO SLOWLY TOO
DONT TOUCH THAT MASK—THE AIR'LL COME THROUGH
STICK TO IT MAN—WITH GAS 'TIS SAID
THERE'S BUT TWO MEN—THE QUICK-THE DEAD"

You feel it lurking always near
Your senses seem its voice to hear
"TAKE OFF YOUR MASK—RELIEVE ITS PAIN
FROM OFF YOUR FACE, AND BREATHE AGAIN."

You want to—here is how it feels
The mouthpiece seems like molten steel
The strained air scarce fills your lungs
Your mouth seems doubly filled with tongues.

Yet on it stays, for hours too
Until the gaseous ghost is through
Until sweet air comes driving in
And no more sounds the shell burst's din.

Then we all say, with eyes still wet
"THANK GOD—ONE MORE ATTACK—SAFE MET."

The Grandfather

The Grandfather, perfectly old, sits amid
the children of his son, readying an evening tale
and smoking his pipe, highball in hand.

Wherever he is is happiness. There falls no silence
but good. And the children are quiet
while he thinks. They hope for a story they love,

the beaver boy who wants to unweave
his parents' careful dam, the clock with no hands
so no one knows to call them in to bed,

or the boy so brave he goes to the middle
of the woods and the mother cries
till Daddy brings him home.

The Grandfather sets down his drink,
gathers them closer to listen to one
that's true, of the day the Hudson's flow

was stilled by ice from here to there
and the barges piled with bricks were crushed
and he and Henry Hughes took sleds

over ridges and floes to pull the shivering boatmen
into the foundry to give them a sturdy drink,
to warm them body and soul.

He warms his own.

The Grandmother frowns as he drains his glass
against the sleepless hours when dark is backdrop
to the tales he never tells

of his troops invisible in shrouds of gas,
wailing unheard in circus of mortar fire.
She knows it's at night he will see his soldier son

so lost in memory of war,
the thickets of Kiska, Italian scarps,
his father can't find him there.

He rests one hand on the head of the child
who's nearest him and lifts his empty glass.
The Grandmother fills it again.

Coda: The Closing

I thought that I forgave
as deeply as forgiveness goes
but there are days I can't absolve
his acquiescent hands

the right decanting
small blue pills into the chalice
of the left

(why can't his fingers place them
singly on his tongue
so he can taste the bitterness in time?)

then right and left in fists
against our needing him
to dial the phone,
unlock his office door,
fingerthroat the poison up —

they open only as he starts to close,
just enough to tap his telegrams to us

> *know you're the only woman*
> *I have ever really loved*
>
> *be proud of your intellect*
>
> *protect your genius*
>
> *just stay sweet*

and then he lets them stroke the dog

I'll miss you, Rolf, my friend

(do they receive his dying head
as Rolfie makes him weep?)

Coda: The Opening

I.

At the top of our hill,
you stretched and stretched
to plant the hoe,
uprooting the shallow remains
of last year's crops,
rhythmic and shaded
against the tentative blue
of a late April upstate sky.

Mom knelt at her garden just below,
worrying annuals in among
the rampancy of iris and phlox
in the part of her world
she could make beautiful.

Still, you went silently
about your work.

Funny, this chore you chose
to do alone. In other ways
you let us build our characters,
mucking the stall,
watering chickens
and feeding the sheep.
But this kind of work,
this growing things
for the hard ahead,
you always did by yourself.

II.

Funny, the day you chose to die,
the one right after Spring arrived
when you might have
rolled the snow fence away
and begun to pitch the rocks
that had grown somehow
in winter's soil.

I wondered why you'd leave
with your garden promising.

But this year I think
I might begin to understand.
Sometimes I feel
something like tired,
my own bones heavy
and wrongness all around.
Last week I felt an urge
to sleep right through
the making wrong things right.

I thought of you, I thought
oh god, you were so tired,
too tired for simple rest,
too tired to try on hope again.
I think I know you only knew
you needed to sleep.
You slept and I swear I hope
the sinking was kind,
like a soft old chair with arms.

Burning a Poem at My Father's Grave

These are the words
I wrote to claim you
from your haunt inside
a tensile coil of memory.

I send them up on fire
to move invisible
through day, spiral
in the draw of emptiness

to touch the curving underside
of night, burn pinholes
in the dark so we can see
the gleaming of your lightened soul.

I borrowed the words
from you. I want
to give them back,
twice birthed,

as much the shape
of your delivery as mine,
and reverent.

Big Delia: Three Short Novels and an Epilogue

Everyone she met fell for her—tired people in the super-market checkout line, waiters, our teachers and friends, the guy who pumped her gas. Her children and husbands adored her even though, when she was seriously irritated, the temperature soared in the room. She was, always had been, generously beautiful. When, under the name of Sissy Page, she went to Princeton masquerading as her younger brother's lovestruck prom date, she carried off a three-day acting turn so perfect that Tommy's reputation as a charmless Freshman was turned on its head.

****

She had a will of iron. She survived the deaths of three husbands and the protracted adolescence of three daughters. Generally speaking, what she legislated happened. We always did our homework, we did our chores with more or less dispatch, and we bowed even to the occasional food outrage. We suffered liverwurst past normal childhood limits; twice, we ate beef tongue. Once, just because she said they were cooked, she got us to dine on raw shrimp. They hung limp from their tails and you could see through them, but "They're fine!" she commanded and we ate. One of us developed hives so large her torso resembled a topographic map of some small continent.

****

She had little respect for authority or irrational convention. A letter to her parents from the Bryn Mawr Dean announced her house arrest after she rappelled her ivy-covered dorm wall to meet a beau after hours. One day, in a hurry, she completed a series of parking maneuvers so close to illegal that the truck driver she'd stymied leaned from his window to offer a curse-laden description of the operation. Leaving us in the car to watch, she strode her small self to where he sat, gave him her index finger, and, to his speechless surprise, enjoined him to "Be polite!" Pooh-poohing osteoporosis and arthritis, she skied, biked and body-surfed into her seventies. She ignored signs of all kinds—anything claiming private property, for example, and those imploring her not to walk her dogs on the golf course. She led assisted living staff on exciting foot chases down the highway, her wheeled walker racketing on ahead of her.

****

She lived up to the suggestion of adventure in the name she died with: Delia Page Marshall Meneely Blatner Pitkin.

My Mother After Dad

Sometimes her anger
was a hungry mouth.
It ate the lesser humans
in the house, sometimes
the smallest daughter
with her shoes
still on.

And if that weren't
enough to make us
hew the line,
when she had reached
the point she couldn't
stomach one more
sorry soul
the hungry mouth
might wolf

she shut that mouth
and swallowed all the anger
that remained.
She swelled
to twice her normal size
and radiated speechlessness.

That was even worse.

My Mother Becoming a Woman

Her suitor's car stopped
halfway up the hilly drive
where dogwood and lilacs
conceal it from home

profiles in silhouette
springing apart
in the glare
of my headlights

mouths still open
tongues retracting
like heads of turtles
in sudden sulk

my mother retrieving
her hand from behind his ear
his hair untidy
a halo of gray

and the girl behind
compelled to confront
that this might be
how she had come about.

My Mother After All

My mother fell a fearsome dowager,
three times a widow, fury
barely dammed behind her eyes.

Beset with children and a crippled
man, she'd waged and lost her early wars
against the drowning of her days

and all our insufficiencies
set anger boiling in her cheeks.
Our teenaged breaches

of her fragile peace
loosed floods that left us stranded
in an unmoored day,

her husbands flailing
in the backwash,
footing undercut.

But then she fell,
a different woman wakening,
her reservoir of fury spilling dry

until my gentled, puzzled mother
had the millpond's eyes,
sunlight silent

in the deeper part, something
quick and silver turning
in the shallow, flashing

into shadow, gone.

Saving Graces

If not for you I'd kill myself,
my mother said the day we buried
Ned. But since you're here I can't.

She'd been a fatal wife, so testified
three figured urns beneath the soil
of graveyards here and there.

Perhaps she'd earned surcease.
We weren't sure if it was guilt
or gladness we should feel.

But she was mother beyond wife
and she must needs survive. We moved
across her to the other side.

Dodi mothered her with teas and soups.
Sarah counseled Buddha's way,
detaching from the bitter bits.

I gave my hands to the back of her neck,
practiced loving I had learned
from my child how to do.

To My Mother, a Child

I remember noons
when I located
by the shape of
you at end of day.
I remember the seasons
sweet on your skin
when you held me hello,
your body young and strong
and all I wished to gather
and be gathered by.

I remember parsing
every detail of your mood,
angling for your smile,
watching for surprise
to light your face
before you laughed.

I felt we were continuous
in times of pure content.

I am not ready for you
fugitive, the way
you fade from me when I
begin to press. I'm crippled
by the film that falls
between us now,
the untold news of days
we occupy apart.
I never thought you'd live
so far behind your eyes.

If a poem can hold
what suffers
between words,
let this one bound
the loss, the difference
between the you in me
and you a secret
in your own opacity.

Reach: The Daughter

At visit's end she floats
half in half out.
I have sung with her
old songs we know.
I have teased her cheeks
with my fingers.
I have mentioned
everything.

In a silence held
a moment too long,
she slips my claim on her,
falls away in sudden sleep,
her head turned sideways
on the wingback chair.
She looks like someone
slapped, dismissed.

But I would say
she's not so much
abandoned as abandoning,
beginning to relinquish me
behind the doors of anterooms
where I can't go.

Reach: The Mother

After dying lures her
into lying down,
all the laughter
she has ever heard
swims back toward her
in chords, the music
measureless and humming
in her blood.

The meter is so strong
against the rhythm
of her heart, her heart
is distracted,
wants to dance
to the deeper beat

and she begins
to cede herself
to laughter's lift
when she knows
she should reach
for her daughter's hand,
hold on to the weight
of staying behind.

It Might Be Like This

for Delia Meneely Pitkin, died 11:17 a.m.

The radio switched off
in mid-cadenza,
notes suspended
in the room and this,
the sounding silence
where they were.

Water slowly thickening
at winter harbor's edge
until an ocean wrinkle
holds as ice.

An image on her eyelids
of a tree against the sun,
light where dark should be,
the opposite of true.

Perhaps like this for her,
the dream she wants to grasp
eluding memory,
circus train retreating
down a narrowing rail
toward a cleft
in the summer hills.

Yes, this: she waking
from a long and riddling
fantasy that slips away,

characters dissolving, meaning
drowned in light

and light her element
as she pulls free of dream
and rumpled sheets
to rise into its width
and clarity.

The Animal Says No

The others called her dying
almost beautiful and wept
the baffled way you do
before a beauty you can penetrate
no more than it can enter you.

What they saw was kind,
the small capitulation
of her final breath,
the end of our wondering
what to wish, her passage
into past so quiet
you could hardly tell.

But none of them was at her bed
the moment when my mother
sat straight up,
hands in fists, her eyes alive
with fury I believed
old age had doused.
It was as if she'd just caught on.

She rose so fast from nearly gone
I had to lean away.
Defying weeks of blur
and lessening,
this momentary mother
of my growing up
came strong with stubbornness,
outrage growling in her throat.

I couldn't find my way
to side with her
before she just as quickly
threw the match, lay back
against her pillows,
died a gentlewoman's death.

I've kept the confrontation to myself.
It was not beautiful.

II. BEDTIME STORIES

Bedtime, 1951

I like to lie awake as light
retreats from our room
and toys along the floor
emerge as memory
of themselves. I like
the velvet weight
of blindness on my eyes.

In the deepening
ache of midsummer
I listen for nightsong
in the wood or wait
for what arises in a quieting,
a growing wind uneasy
in the longer grass,
the rain beginning blunt
and noisy on the eaves
then purling in the gutter pipe.

Downpour tatters.
The center of the storm blows on
and silence moves toward the house
from underneath the trees.
In the bunk below me,
Sarah sighs, asleep. Alone,
I yield to rhythms surfacing,
carried as a part of rabbits
breathing in the field,
night birds falling through the air.

Bedtime, 1981:
If I Wanted, Now I Could Give Myself

a wind to skim the coolness at rest on the river,
  carry it up to my attic room,
  lay it along my stomach and thighs

a strength of light to stem the leak of darkness
  from its lairs in furrows of sheet
  and widening ceiling cracks

music enough inside to mute the sound
  of pointed, double-bodied wasps
  that spiral unevenly, malign and foolish with heat

Mother seated by my bed, sending her voice
  around the room to tame the looming furniture,
  caress the sour arthritic cat asleep on a book

a cradle of sleep to catch my fall, warm and rhythmic
  with my breath, a half-familiar solitude
  I'd come from formed and rightful every day.

Diminution: Toward Silence

My friend began to disappear
in our Junior year,
melting at every softness
to thinly covered curve of bone.
Our teachers frowned
as she lost her way
and she gazed back at them
through a strange translucency.

In her greenstone house,
on its acres of shadowed fields,
with creek and setters
and ruminant cows,
her room lay out toward silence,
almost enclosed by the dark
and breath of the hills.
Together there we could
have spoken of everything,
but the words she offered
were empty of her:
whatever consumed her
was sucking away at truth.

Years later, persuaded again
to eat and institutional shadows
fading beneath her eyes,
she told me: *he came to my bed
the nights when you weren't there.*

I wish for her that every time
he'd pushed me back
from the front porch door

and kissed me, his tongue
a creature probing
the wall of my teeth,
furtively moving along my gums,

I wish I had let the fury fork
from my mouth,
watched his face turn brittle
and break, his lips fly loose
as they tried to recapture
the unsexed tongue.

But I only watched
as she tried to journey back
to where she was no more
than a gleam in her father's eye.

Diminution: Bereaved

She never says a word the nights he leaves
their bed, often as she reaches out
to touch his back. She's learned to sleep bereaved.

He cannot think that she is so naïve
as not to know. She's simply swallowed shut.
She never says a word the nights he leaves.

She has to leave her daughter to retrieve
herself. She will not know if Father taught
to touch him back. She's learned to sleep bereaved.

Her daughter has to find a way to live
the after days. Each morning you forget.
She never says a word the nights he leaves

although he twists the blankets when he heaves
himself to bed where she has lain without
his touch. He's back. She's learned to sleep bereaved.

While he is gone, she lets her body grieve
for heat and sweetening she's come to doubt.
She never says a word the nights he leaves
to touch behind her back. She sleeps bereaved.

Ménage à Trois

You always say you're sorry
you can't sleep if I'm too close,
sorry that you have to face away
to view your dreams.
Like loving me, your sleeping
is a private careful thing.

But now I see you rise from dream,
arms stretched out into the dark,
sheets unwinding from your narrow chest.
You cry out joy or protest, I can't tell.
In case it's joy, I do not interrupt,
reluctant to be found alongside
what you've lost.

The Stranger in My Bed

I. My Bed

I used to love the way sleep
harbored me, whispered me in
with voices overheard—
grief of the wind shut out,
murmur of snowfall in the field,
rain's tattoo on the hardwood leaves.
I loved the way dark closed on me
in the flow of summer night,
the way sleep wound
inside the flickering of thoughts
and swallowed them for dream,
leaving me only myself
in her sweet loose hold,
the fragrant wrap of sun-dried sheets.

II. The Clerk at the Starlite Motel

The quiet must have quivered
as he slid between the wall and me,
but somehow I slept on until
he was a solid shadow
tight against my back,
husk around a soft inside.
I stirred, he caught my right hand
in his right, pressed the noise
of my surprise into the pillow
with his left. I understood.

Without a sound I let him
raise and lower what I wore,
force the silence into me,
steal rhythm of my sleeping breath,
make it insistent, wrong.

I couldn't guess how
something like this ends
and when at last I didn't care,
he stopped, mistaking
my abandonment for fellowship.
He spoke of life in bed at home.

Later in the day, I told
his story to the ER staff.
You needn't swab, I said:
his trouble is he can't get off.
My weapon was in listening.
He thanked me when he left.

III. The Troopers

The troopers braked
just short of bumping
in the parking lot,
carnival and portent
in the alternating lights.

Grey hats low across their eyes,
their faces stone,
they questioned me

while I maintained a kind of truth:
I hadn't seen his face.

They searched and dusted,
stripped the sheets.
I think you know, they said.
I did, but I was afraid.
I'd written everything he'd need
to hunt me down.

At last the older trooper
sat beside me on the naked bed,
laid his hat across his thighs.
Please say, he said, for women
in the neighborhood.
And I gave in again.
He thanked me, too.

IV. It Felt Like Love I Felt

While I was in the witness box
my troopers radiated duty
and a quiet tenderness my way.
They testified, bareheaded
but undoubtable, to fingerprints
on both sides of the door
and bruises noted in the doctor's file.
When the jurors filed back in,
permitting news to travel
toward us in their eyes,
my troopers nodded, proud of me.

V. The Stranger in My Bed

I lay so deep in sleep's familiar curve
I felt too late the alteration
of the air, the shaping
of the night's hands into his.
He borrowed me from sleep
and left me separate
so I became
the stranger in my bed,
odd, ungentle, wrong.

In Winterbed

We burrow in the dips
our bodies deepen
every year. On your side
there is quiet,
ruck of blanket rising
and falling at your ear.
I lie awake, tossing
the day for poetry.

You sleep in a simplicity,
streetlight on your cheek.
All I have to do is reach
across the little mountain
we have made and you
will turn toward me,
your big hand drawing me
through cold to custody.

Catness: On Being Good in Bed

After the restless heft of you
I love the cat's small weight
against my leg,
her nickel's worth of warmth.

After the plaint and shiver
of your dreams, I love
the even rise and fall
of her calico haunch.

After waking to your face
still marked with trouble
even sleeping can't erase,
I love the hum that says
my loving her
is perfect and enough.

Catness: My Husband Is Not a Cat

He's not a cat
though like a cat
in bed he wants sometimes

to fit himself into my curve
and other times
to sleep a space apart

and there were times
before his war fell back
behind the years

he'd mew the grief
of a surviving warrior
in early morning dreams.

He's not a cat. He never purrs.
Without that it is hard to know
his healing is complete.

Two-Part Invention

We're napping after lunch
while Tom the carpenter
makes downstairs right.
The afternoon is musical:
Tom is sawing, Gary snores,
their rhythms soft and regular.

But Tom deploys a drill.
Gary's stertor stops
without his wakening.
The drill relents and Gary,
testing silence in his sleep,
begins his song anew.

The drill-bit bites
another board and once again
my husband stills, asleep.
I have to turn away to laugh,
this manly counterpoint
sostenuto sotto ma non troppo.

Spiderwork

On cold dry nights,
something arachnid
visits my sleep.
When I stretch my arms
into the day,
I see webs have been spun
on the backs of my hands,
a tatting of fine white threads.

I accept how my skin
has turned quiet.
I'm touched
by the papery slide of it
over my bones,
the way it is fragile
and heals itself,
the softness it secrets
in gullies and dents.

I'm grateful
for how it stretched
to house my child
and I don't mind
the deep impress
of laughter
around my mouth.

I love how it stipples
with pleasure
of touch or song.

But some mornings
my hands seem to wear
the warp and the weft
of somebody's shroud.

Simple Absence

Dad was
the moon falling.

A shining falling moon
describes not merely
simple absence in the sky
but beauty changing,
something lovely turning
terrible with flight.

The dream releases me
before I see
the moon in puddles
at a flat place.

III. WEATHERING

Weather Whys: A Short Memoir

Where I grew up, people shook their heads and sighed: oh, our weather. Albany sat in a declivity dug by eons of the Hudson's flow, surrounded by mountains, the Adirondacks and elderly Catskills looming to the north and south, Helderbergs and Berkshires to the west and east. The weather that collected there was likely to stay for a while, long February cold snaps matched by merciless heat waves in July. In fall and spring we lived under a cloud canopy I never noticed till I moved my Louisiana-born husband northward for a brief spell in what he called perpetual shade.

So I can be forgiven for believing that the weather actually was ours, wholly produced by my hometown, rising from the land itself. I believed further and faithfully that Albany made its weather in an evenhanded way, bad weather lasting only so long before it was replaced with something better. And Albany was proof against outside influence: if the sky boiled over Poughkeepsie while we bathed in sun, why, that was Poughkeepsie's decision and nothing to do with us.

Sadly, after years of meteorological vigilance as a member of FEMA's Response and Recovery staff, I'm wise now to El Niños and La Niñas, isobars and cold fronts and blocking highs. I have to accept that the weather we refer to as "ours" is no more ours than time or air. It visits from somewhere else and then moves on. If we want to know what kind of storm may hit us on Tuesday, we need to start paying attention to Oklahoma on Saturday. The clouds above us now may visit again after circling the entire globe.

I love the science and drama and mystery of weather, the way it rolls and cycles, binds each of us to all of us. I'm grateful for the foreknowledge that has me scrambling to mobilize lanterns, fill my bathtub and reorganize my closets (don't ask) for days before the storm arrives. But I miss the weather that belonged to me. Whether it rose sweet or terrible, Mom and Dad would manage. They always did.

Summer Written Back

June

Morning is three walls we wake to
on the summer sleeping porch.
The price of nights out here
is silence till the adults wake
and we're reduced to wordless
poking between beds.
We wait as told, listen
to the shuddering of Sunday
in the church next door.
The adults slumber
through the early services.

July

Dad perspires with tilling
so his vegetables can breathe
and curses ardently the drought,
the rabbits and the deer.
Inside, we find the cool
in nooks where awnings
close the day to dusk.
The rooms dream
underwater dreams.

August

Morning's dazzle
in my mother's garden
yields to midday dark
and steady rain comes warm.
Purpleblue hydrangeas
quicken from their droop,
grasses soften and the well refills.
Mom and Dad are serene
as life turns good
and we're allowed this once
to dance outside
without our clothes.

Reading Signs

Shadows of the dunes
have not yet crept
across the upper beach
but no one's here.
A neon pail, tiny crabs
still scrabbling in its well,
leans inside a furrow
in the sand.

I see the way it went:
At noon the parents walked
and laughed too far,
their fingers greedy
in the children's hair.
The sky flared
and the breeze, salt-
pungent, blew onshore,
pushing mounds of spume
against their feet.
Moaning the cold,
they bullied out
to ride the waves
that excited the skin
on their bellies and thighs.
The children rolled
in the undertow's
pleasurable pull.

By two, the tide's retreat
had left a glimmering
of jellyfish. Tomato sandwiches

had barely served,
the drinks were warm,
the chocolate compromised
by grit. The parents' need
to touch their children's skin,
to hold them small
inside their colored towels,
was satisfied.

By three the sky had widened
until blue was agony,
the wind's insistence
a slender knife.
Something wild hung coiled
inside the children's shouts.
The parents had begun
to stalk the end
of afternoon.

At four the parents
closed their faces up
and left. The children
understood they wouldn't
find them anymore,
condensed themselves,
forgot what shapes they'd been
and disappeared
inside the afternoon.

I Becoming a Woman

When Hank pulled me
to the bottom
of the darkwater pond
I was genuinely shocked:
I'd thought it was Leigh
he liked.

She wasn't exactly beautiful
but Leigh sent messages,
my mother said. Boys
were pulled to the edge
of her heat and hung there
waiting to be beckoned in.
Hank, exempt from competition
with these males of lesser
tans and pectorals,
observed with a smile
of fledgling irony.
I was audience to it all.

Leigh and I raced the length
of the dock and jumped
from different sides. Hank dove
beneath us, swam toward me,
stores of air in his athlete lungs.
I was just beginning to beat
toward light when he circled
my ankle with his hand
and drew me down.
I jerked my legs to tell him
I had let my own air bubble out,

pried at his hand with my other foot
and felt him catch it, too. I clawed
to drag us up but we were
one long body sliding back.
My chest was just about
to suck the silted water in
when he let go.

If I kicked at his head when I thrust
through the lid of the pond,
I was filled with forgiveness
when he surfaced, smiling,
next to me.
On the splintered dock
my best friend Leigh
stood peevish and alone,
one arm across her midriff,
knuckles furrowing her lower lip.
Hank had chosen me to drown.
I could have died of happiness.

Backhand

We played on the macadam court
that sang the landing of a truly righteous shot
and amplified the English
we put on an evil stroke.

Partners, we were nearly equal
in all things. Nearly. Almost. Truth:
in all things she outplayed me, tennis,
bridge, couture and hair control and boys.

And yet I felt not humble, nor did I love her less.
We shared. One year she let her boyfriend
teach me how to kiss. One year we double-dated
with one boy. We lived as if in "ours".

And yet. We never said our fathers drank
to sodden sloppiness. We never spoke
the sometimes shame. I never knew
she didn't sleep, she didn't know I couldn't eat.

One day I told her Dad had killed himself
and she returned my serve, a backhand shot
I couldn't reach: "You are the lucky one,"
she said, "I envy you."

With George: Sunday in Park

There is a space
alongside George,
an angled invitation made
by his careless ready arm
on the long seatback
and his torso, warm
beneath an ironed shirt.
As he drives, I slide in increments
to join him there.
He smells like a man,
like my father
in the mornings, clean
and intentional.

I love his hand when he
drops it to my arm
and tucks me in,
the way he steers
with a single palm,
the bunch and slide
of his muscles
when he works the car
into a hidden overlook.

I love the easy way
he lifts me to kiss,
the tilt of my face
under his,
the curve of my neck,
his big sly thumb

moving slowly in circles
under my ear.

But I hardly breathe,
careful to bring
no other part
of myself to its notice,
the circling thumb
that already knows
the give of my skin,
the slope to my collarbone.

With George: Some Days

The mail slides in, as usual, by two.
As usual, there's nothing there of you
except the magazine my old school sends
to keep a bead on all its friends with cash
to spare now that their kids are grown and gone.
I could, I guess, pick up the phone.

But it was always you who made the call.
You were the guy and all I had to do
was follow where you led. You'd take me slow,
you said, and so you did, not furthest I would
go, of course, but furthest I had been.
Above the falls that night, I could have thought
of sin, but all I had inside my head
was spooling silk. You said it was all right.
I fell into your voice, your hand so sweet
I barely felt it disassembling choice.
I simply let my muscles melt.

We haven't kissed since nineteen sixty-two
but it is you I don't consign to past
and done. You were the first, perhaps the only
one who knew how little it would take
to wake my skin. When even now I smell
your aftershave, I let you in.

Einstein's River

So everyone I've ever been
is back there on the river
alone in the moment
she occupies,
watching the eddy
of time around her feet,
the way her having to be there
stutters the forward flow of hours.

I'm not unhappy they're out of sight
beyond the backward curve,
the girl who squeezes
wanting everything
into a laugh
that sounds like chalk,
the one with breasts beginning
to nudge her white ribbed undershirt
who verges on confessing sins of thought.

Through river fog, I peer ahead
to spy the women I will be
grown smaller and pale
as the hours bend,
smiling one,
sorrowing one, hands
upraised in prayer or outcry,
fingers lifted to blame and caress.

And here's the woman filled with the ones behind
breathing the ones ahead like genies from her mouth.

She's holding this poem, asks only
that the blue-tongued wind
lick free the words
and drop them
where the water's roil
will weave the lines into a raft
to float the curves and eddies on.

I Love My Self

that plucked from Dad's
back shelf the five slim albums
I could take with me to college.
Their covers called to me.

When Mom and Dad had driven off,
my yellow rug and matching spread
installed, my brand new record player
by the bed, I stacked the albums,
watched the miracle of drop
and arm and groove,
and listened
while I smoked a Winston
like a grownup girl.

Stravinsky's Firebird
was a shock.
How little I knew, my
self back then,
how happy I was,
half-formed, with little reason
to suspect.
How much I loved a coffee
with my cigarette,
the lyrical noise
of women in the hall.
How much I loved the way
my door could open to the hive
or close me wholly in.
How close we grew,

my records five and I.
How marvelous they stacked
and dropped and dropped
and dropped
while I learned more than anyone needs
of eighteenth century literature.

If you play me any of them
now, wherever we are
will disappear.

The Real World: Four Short Novels

Right after graduation, I moved to a Vermont town so small
one went "down-street" to the shopping area (a grocery store,
a laundromat, and a jewelry repair shop run by a graduate of
the town's only real industry, the State mental hospital) and
"up-street" to the high school, the billiards hall and the town
swimming pool, available during July and August to natives who
found "recently melted" a pleasant water temperature. I went
there to ski and, between weekends, to teach. But by the end of
my first day as the new Waterbury High School English teacher,
I knew I'd found in the classroom one of my favorite places in
the world.

At 7:45 on the first Tuesday in September, 1965, fresh from 18
years of single-sex education, I faced my first coeducational class,
the A Seniors. To their startlement—and my own (I was flying
on instruments)—I established a pattern I would follow every
day that year, bidding them stand until invited to sit and calling
the roll formally: Mr. Grace, Miss Izzo, Miss MacLeod, Mr.
Sabin.

Dreams of small counter-offensives danced in their heads.

I was well into a brief overview of our prospective adventure
in World Literature when Donald Merchant, a sweet-faced kid
with a blond crew-cut, sneezed loudly from the back row. As he
sneezed, he spoke to me and what he said was, "HORSEshit!"
With the perfect dumb luck of the pedagogically untutored, I
laughed, as, after a moment, did everyone else in the room, first
the boys and then the girls. The first period of every day went
right after that, every single day.

****

After my first two weeks, the principal, Mr. Hoskiewicz, observed one of my classes for evaluation purposes. Several days later, he called me into his office for a conference. Everything was fine, he said, with just two corrections to be made: I must not respond to my students with any affirmative except "yes"—my "yups" and "yeahs" were poor influences; and I must teach from behind my desk. By way of persuasion, he told me a story. He'd been walking down the hall one day behind Tommy Gibbs and Tommy Guyette. He'd heard Tommy Gibbs ask Tommy Guyette what he thought of that new English teacher. "Well," Tommy Guyette had said, "she's all right I guess, but when she sits up on that desk and crosses her legs, it shakes me up some." I learned to teach standing up.

****

I lived in the apartment over Jack Patterson's garage. Jack also owned the trailer park behind the garage. Francis Hanson, eight years old, lived there with his mother. He and I used to ride my motorcycle around the hills on Saturdays, he everlastingly grateful that I let him wear the helmet. When the World's Fair opened in Montreal, the math teacher and I thought we'd take Francis. He was dazzled by the sheer size of things, the spread of the spectacle. But the last exhibit we visited had to do with WWII. When we entered the tent, we fell straight into the middle of a movie about the death camps. After a short time, Francis looked up at me entreatingly. Could we move along? We did. Halfway through the walk to the car, Francis said, simply, "I don't think that's something a good little Catholic boy should see." He was the best little Catholic boy I ever met.

****

David Giles didn't make trouble but he regarded me with the heavy-lidded near-insolence of the Sophomore class heartthrob. He didn't have much in the way of a family life, as near as I could tell, but on Parents' Night, he slid into my classroom late in the evening with his brother. Donnie, trim in his Army uniform and emanating David's musky self-assurance, chatted with me briefly and, on his way out, told me he'd see me around.

What happened next didn't get back to me for several months, not until after I'd parted company with Paul Bean, the broad-shouldered local draftsman who gave me his grandmother's TV and took me to Montpelier every Sunday afternoon for a hamburger and a milkshake and a kiss. The night I had to tell Paul I wasn't the marrying kind, I didn't know of the debt I owed him. He'd been at the bar in the billiards hall on Parents' Night when Donnie Giles stopped in. He was still there, some beers later, when Donnie announced that he could "have" that English teacher "anytime he wanted." Paul Bean lifted him off his barstool by his khaki lapels and offered to help him revise his opinion or the arrangement of his face, either one.

I didn't deserve Paul Bean, and he agreed. I only saw him once after I turned his proposal down, just for a minute when he retrieved his grandmother's TV. But he couldn't undo his singular defense of my honor, unwrite the small-town legend we became.

October, Vermont

Fall comes in
    aslant (though not miserly
       or thin like other biases)

the longest slope
    in afternoons when light
       slips down the nearer hills

angles through my window,
    cleaving clean through
       noon's leftover thrum.

What They Know: The Sophomore Boys

Shy Mr. McIntosh, big
and slowly softening,
used himself up
for college ball,
fell into life
as a high school coach.
Good-natured, good-looking
and slightly at sea,
he paces the field
and the echoing gym
on feet of incongruous modesty.

Miss Fontella is barely contained
by the office where she guides
the Sophomore boys,
has outsized feet
and thighs that shush each other
when she walks.
New York City born and bred,
she talks in stereophonic bursts
with a cheerleader's certainty.
Her laugh creates silence
like blasphemy in church.

Fontella has McIntosh
square in the crosshairs
of her love. When they pass
in the halls, her eyes slide left
and she crowds the center line,
transmitting heat.
He does not slow but sunburn

rises on his neck.
The older faculty, solid
in their otherness,
pouch their mouths
and look away.

But the Sophomore boys
do not need to resist
the images of woman and man
engaged in a dance
of tussle and heave,
buttocks afloat like moons
reflected on a tumbled sea,
legs like water beasts,
breaking the surface,
submerging again,
his feet submissive to hers.

The Sophomore boys
are not afraid
of the nakedness
under their teachers' clothes,
the bloom of satiety
on their cheeks.

What They Know: The Cheerleaders

It's what they summon
of their sex,
the way they've learned so early
to dissemble ecstasy,
arms and legs flung wide
in manufactured glee.

It's what they know
of manhood, mostly
sweat, untutored fingers
asking entry at
zippers and pleats
in the back seat of the bus,
hands less cherishing
than those they see caress
the basketball,
deliver it and hold
the memory of its shape
with careful grace.

It's what they know
of disappointment, almost
guessing that it dogs the years
and breaks the boys
who disappoint.
They give themselves regardless
in the harsh and selfless angles
only puppeteers should ask.

Solstice

Just outside the entrance
to the underground
a frozen ravening man
hurls his voice into the crowd
of passersby. He says
we're no damned good.

It's true we're barely generous
inside our scarves and gloves.
It's five o'clock.
Our wallets are a satisfaction
we can heft against
the longest evening of the year.

A woman who commutes
in heels pauses
in front of him and hurries on.
We follow her, eyes down,
a single herd he can't unthread.

Beyond his voice, we separate,
revealed each to the rest.
We minimize inside
the early dark, concise,
complex and unaccountable.

The Single Woman, Twenty-Eight

I was tending someone else's house
which smelled of winter and dying plants
when my appendix burst. I felt myself
go wrong but the white-haired men
would only shake their heads.
They said it was the woman's cramps.

Where do women go?

I said to my mother I have crawled
to the phone I smell of dying plants.

Do they go home to mother?

She said you must believe the men your
father was a doctor and we should have
known he'd burst as winter died.

Do they have to have fathers?

She said you mustn't crawl your father
left us standing up you do not see us
crawling after him.

Do they always go halfway?

At last she said she'd come. I waited
out the hours in a silent room my
woman's body flexed around a childlike
pain and gave myself a cradling dry
sweet song. I chanted *mummy
mummy mummy*.

When it is time do they carry
their cramps through the kitchen
down the hallways into quiet parlors
by the dying plants quietly?

Do they offer to make lunch,
to die of gratitude?

Flying Out

On the night-filled street
below my room, a pointed noise
careens toward center town
and I am sucked into its wake,
a flying figure out of bed.
All that I have on sings off,
the bedclothes first
and then the things I was
today: woman
thinking at her desk,
mother searching
mirrors for her mother
leaking through, writer
combing her own debris
for clues to how we mean.

Air and cold are fingers
working at the knots
I've made in all my limbs
and loosening the grasp
of those who cling
like shame to places
where I bend
till they are dancing
in my slipstream
disappearing, gone,
and I am clean and narrow,
whistling on alone,
horizontal to the winter sky
and home.

The Rhythms Gone Awry

Night makes the maternity ward
a waiting place of slow surprise.
Birth and death transpire
in time that spirals down
toward moments that will
alter everything.

I alone am wakeful in this room,
Two other mothers stir uneasily,
helpless in the flow of hours
toward dawn, trying in sleep
to still a faulty urgency.
A third is feverish, lies clenched
around her pregnancy.

There's something wrong
with all of us, the rhythms
gone awry.

I see my child a girl
and day by day I slip
toward loving her.
I'm vigilant tonight, deciding
again against the urge
to carry her.
What if I closed around her
while I slept?

She'd suffer the loss
of one of us.
We've used our union up,
strangers to each other

and ourselves and both
a little mad.

And who is she
but me and him
in one conjugal impulse,
joyless and direct?

I make her will my own.
Tomorrow I will take her
into preternatural sleep
and leave her there
while I depart this waiting place
bereft and freed, my body
and my dreams
both empty and my own.

The Underground: Five Notes

Public transportation in the nation's capital is the ultimate in movable feasts, bounteous aboveground and below.

Above you have the advantage of being able to see your drivers. From first encounter, you can gauge pretty well the likely quality of your trip. Drivers who open cheerfully to you are more likely to take their time en route, satisfied to stay in lane regardless of their forward progress. The ones who barely suffer you to board often provide more exciting commutes, whaling in and out of traffic, accelerating to sudden stops inches short of pedestrians in their aggravating crosswalks.

And they're the central performers in the traveling show. They play the lead in the not infrequent drama of the driver and the passenger who, perspiring whiskey, wants to steady himself against the front pole, too uncertain to walk farther back and showing signs that he might throw up. They also provide moments of sweet melodrama. One winter day, the taller of two small boys gives my driver some money. What about him, she asks, pointing to the smaller boy. The boys simply watch her, expressionless. She pauses, waves both of them on, reaching into her purse for something she drops into her transparent money box. A man stops on the white line alongside her and says, *I love you, baby, you got good blood.*

****

Underground, as I have said, we know not to whom we entrust our lives. Occasionally an operator will address us directly: we'll be underway again when a faulty signal is fixed; we may be stalled under the river for a while as officials clear a crime in the station ahead. Sometimes, though, we simply wait in unenlightened silence. Once, very early one morning, my train sails through two stops without either deceleration or any word of explanation. It is clear to me for seven long minutes that our driver has died.

****

But the Metro is hands down the best way to get where you want to go in DC, unmetaphorically speaking, anyway. Aboveground, the ride is fraught with fits and starts; city noise presses in from every side and the bus itself squeals, passes wind, hisses and growls. Metro trains move nearly soundlessly on balloon tires through tiled and spacious caverns. They're generally on schedule. The weather is many levels above.

Underground, of course, we have only ourselves for amusement. But we are our own variety show. We are the good-tempered extroverts; we are the resolutely separate. We are the Type-A locals; we are the relaxed, blond nuclear families from Minnesota. We are the bureaucrats with our accordion folders; we are the students muscling human-sized backpacks through the crowd and speaking what might be Korean or Farsi. Sometimes, there rides a person more interesting than all the others put together: a small man with matted hair and an air of sanctimony, for example, raises a brass horn to his lips after every stop and blows taps.

****

The best time to travel underground is the hour before the regular morning commute. The trip is quick. At many stops there is no one on either side of the doors and they open to slap shut again almost without pause. Recently sprung from sleep, we are not even roused fully by the invisible woman who exhorts us PLEASE to stand clear of the doors. One morning I watch a commuter grope in her purse, pull out a brush, remove her headphones, give her hair a thorough working over and repeat the sequence backwards without ever opening her eyes. On the five-thirty a.m. train from Bethesda, a tailored businessman stands mid-car, arm hooked around one of the center poles. He is snoring.

****

The best thing about the dawn commute is the hush, every car a traveling study hall. People are mostly sleeping or reading the same four books. In the 1960s high school study halls I proctored, those were *Lord of the Flies, A Separate Peace, Romeo and Juliet* and *The Red Badge of Courage.* On the train, in my era, it is the latest John Grisham or Tom Clancy or Michael Crichton or the Bible.

I love these little out-of-time interludes in the work day, wonderful for reading and for observing the other underside of Washington, D.C., the one that never makes Meet the Press.

Regretting Spring: Not Spring Again

Southern spring comes in admiring herself and promising
warmth she can't provide, leans halfway over
the backyard fence as if to settle below

(where the raw black soil, laid open by my husband's hand
and closed again with sleeping seed inside,
lies scarred and puckered, the good still underneath)

leans almost to touch and pulls back, beguiling
and cold. We wait unsure while she hesitates
and then she comes as a prodigal

using the whole year's color up for the yellow burn
of forsythia, the iris' purple tongue, the tender
garish lawn. Before we wake

she clarifies the mornings to transparency,
and afternoons she gathers light
to keep the night apart, lays balm of air

on our shoulders and arms. We give ourselves up
to the lulling and drape of the days and then
she sashays out, laughing at us

as summer, big with heat and humorless,
passes in to face a trail of lily sticks, papery curls
of daffodil, sallow pansies, toppled peonies.

And just as the seasons cross, spring reaches back,
releases the dark she's held aside,
lets night swing slowly shut.

Regretting Spring: Fall Catalogues

In any case, in fraying gardens,
green's retreat from leaf and lawn
and minutes falling off the light
at dinnertime, September makes us wonder
if we misremember all that flowed
and billowed out of May.

And this September promises
to slam the summer shut.
In mackerel skies, sudden pauses
in the insects' shrill, periodic shivers
in the crowns of sycamores
and slight bewilderments of sense,
we read the news that a storm,
her belly full of hot Saharan cloud,
is glancing off the southern coast
and veers toward D.C.,
daylight pulsing in her wake.

Resigned, we face her likely thefts:
at least the undertended annuals
that trail from planters on our porch,
at worst the weakest sycamore;
at least the underhum of traffic on the pike,
at worst the way from anywhere to here;
at least the light of day, at worst
the light of lamps deployed
against the infiltrating dark.

But there is loss in any case,
in summer's ebb, the muted birdsong,

morning's lesser cherishing.
In any case, we might concede
that May and June are always
partly for regret.

2001: The Poet's Work for D.C. If a Bomb

FEMA instructions, Fall 2001: Be ready to
remain at your desks.

If you should be the one who's left
to document the flattened capital,
memorials a memory and heat
still caught below a thickened sky,

if you are left to hear the howls
of orphans in the suburbs
as the city nullifies,
their parents borne toward them
in cloud of something
less than dust,

if quiet should enclose a city
where the sirens used to sound
and traffic flowed importantly,
Metro mumbling
underneath the babel of democracy,

if night should fall on nothing
in the streets

it will be up to you
to write the monody,
deliver it beside the Monument
condensed to headstone on the Mall.

Heard Poem

My first day off since 9/11
I join the women
swarming unfamiliar aisles
of hardware stores, lost amid
the ranks of mantools, snatching
what remains of duct tape,
plastic sheets to seal
our windowed rooms,
and masks for gas.
The enemy, we overhear,
has trained his rage
on nearby real estate
and we will count
as pure collateral reward.
Ahead of me, a D.C. Woman,
crisp and coiffed,
talks of weather
to her mother far away,
fingers jigging on her cell.
Her chatter masks the fright
she isn't sure is justified.
Remember, Mom, she says,
I love you. I will call again
tomorrow if I can.

The Unreal World: One Short Story

It is mid-December of 2001 and I am seated at the dinner table with 13 members of my family. We are the motley crowd found at many holiday tables: the quiet, the hilarious, the older and the younger, the leaders and the followers.

But this family is only temporary, its members a FEMA emergency support team deployed to a remote facility in a period of heightened terrorist alert. Our task is to plan for the aftermath of an attack on the National Mall and, from this safe distance, to manage response to its devastation.

Each of us has his or her personal life largely invisible to the others. Many nights, we retreat to our monastic rooms for our 10 hours alone, pursuing interests that might bore the rest of us to tears. But for the 12 hours we share, we find ways to interpret ourselves in a common language, fit ourselves into the jigsaw puzzle of our group, altering personal angles if necessary to make the melding work. We have our differences—but for now we're more alike than not.

We're all afraid. We are tired past the point where we can distinguish one degree of fatigue from another. We focus on planning for the aftermath of horror, resolutely avoiding any conversation about its consequences for us. We may be angry in some subterranean way we keep separate from our will to work.

We are lonesome for our loved ones, terrified we might survive them in a terrorist event, an unthinkable possibility we can't stop thinking about. Silently we search ourselves for answers to a question only King Solomon could deal with: if the alarms go off for a terrorist attack on the DC area, how will we choose between 1) performing our critical professional tasks and 2) leaving our posts as fast as possible to find our families, move them to safety or die with them? This is the kind of thinking that makes you weep.

So what we do is to laugh. We laugh at each other. We laugh at the jokes we tell, their subtlety diminishing in direct proportion to the extension of our time here. More often as the weeks go by, we gather in the evening to laugh at the movies we rent from the local video store. We laugh at ourselves.

And we pat each other's shoulders as we pass, squeeze each other's arms during difficult meetings, offer and receive the occasional hug. We share snacks. Sometimes, as we collect at night with our pizza and the Dr. Dolittle 2 tape, we are completely content. In a way, we love each other.

There are times at the end of unusually long days when I feel more connected with ourselves than I do with the family I left at home. For the first time, I understand my husband's feeling about the members of the squadron with whom he flew in Vietnam. We are all we have just now—and under the circumstances, that's turned into more than enough.

How to Lose a Government Job: Three Short Notices

I.

It was too late to retract my offer.

It was Friday afternoon and I'd gotten word that morning
that the White House had scheduled a Monday Rose Garden
ceremony to celebrate the good work of FEMA and two other
small Federal agencies. Customer testimonials were to be
the centerpiece of this occasion. My job was to find FEMA's
customer.

All day I'd been calling those FEMA customer service survey
respondents who'd signaled willingness to submit to a follow-
up interview. My job was to locate someone who met a set of
specific criteria: s/he must have suffered serious consequences of
a natural disaster, physical injury included, if possible; s/he must
be grateful to FEMA; s/he must be articulate and willing to
make a short speech to all the members of Congress. S/he must
be willing to travel to DC in two days' time.

After a morning of fruitless phone calls, I found the perfect
person. She adored President Clinton; she was extremely verbal;
she loved FEMA. And her dog had run out into the street during
an earthquake and died when a car struck him. Was she willing
to get on a plane on Sunday for a Monday engagement? "Are you
kidding me?" she asked. "Are you telling me I'm going to meet
Bill Clinton? Are you telling me to piss my chair?"

I felt a vast misgiving but, as I said, it was too late to retract the
offer.

She arrived duly at my office on Monday morning. She was all of five feet tall in her stilettos, and her ponytail dropped below her waist. She was not happy with either her hotel or the taxi ride over. Her eight-year-old granddaughter was glued to her hip. Her husband, a staunch Republican, had elected to stay behind.

In the Rose garden, we sat on bleachers behind a raised platform on which sat Mssrs. Clinton and Gore, the latter with his ankle in a cast. All of us faced a sea of elected officials, John Glenn, for example, front and center. The ceremony moved smoothly forward through two mildly interesting agency presentations and associated customer encomia. And then FEMA's turn came. An agency official spoke movingly of FEMA's role in restoring crippled citizens to wholeness. And our disaster victim was called forward to the microphone at the front of the platform.

"I am a victim of the earthquake in California," she said. "I love FEMA. And I'm not wearing my Depends, but I wish I were."

A brief, stunned silence fell on the crowd. Clinton leaned toward Gore and asked, "What did she say???" Gore responded, "She says she forgot her Depends."

Beyond them, John Glenn lurched forward in his seat, his mouth a perfect "o." And then a wave of laughter came from the back of the crowd and incorporated him.

She continued. I don't know what she said. I was calculating how we would live on one salary. When she finished, a second surprise cemented my sense of doom: her little grandchild, who had an avowed crush on Clinton, ran suddenly from the bleachers to join him as he hugged her grandmother. Four men in dark suits and sporting handguns emerged from nowhere and ran after her. She eluded them, darted up the steps to the dais and flung her arms around the President's legs. Startled and then smiling, Clinton accepted her embrace and the secret service melted back into whatever positions they'd held before.

As it turned out, I, too, was permitted to melt back into my position. No one, apart from half a dozen local reporters, mentioned the incident. Maybe Congress has a big sense of humor; maybe they do not dismiss Depends.

II.

I was leading a group of Federal, State and local staff through an evaluation of the Oklahoma City bombing operation. All players had done an exemplary job in this recovery, and partnerships had flourished.

As usual, FEMA had rented both meeting and sleeping rooms in a local hotel and had contracted for coffee and tea to be provided several times a day. The deliveries were prompt, the beverages hot, the staff solicitous. We felt well taken care of.

But at the end of our last day, as I collected closing comments from participants, the door behind the group opened slowly. The hotel manager appeared, finger to his lips, and ushered in two huge rolling trays of finger food, fresh fruit and vegetables, pastries, hot appetizers, unbelievable bounty.

This was strictly illegal. We were the Feds, bound to accept no such gifts. But, in a short, emotional speech, the manager explained that this was what they must do to express gratitude for the speedy and compassionate response they'd received from our organizations.

When the manager fell silent, he wasn't the only one wiping at tears. All of us in that room had been fighting waves of sorrow and anger and disbelief throughout the week: we had never gotten used to the idea of that kind of deliberate devastation. But it had opened all of us up, and we were as ready for human beauty as ever we would be. Chatting with hotel staff, we ate the contraband, with a quick kind of love I still feel today.

III.

The surest way to lose a government job is to be killed in some outlandish fashion.

We'd had quite enough of being scared. In the Fall of 2001, the possibility of a dirty bomb on the Mall was the talk of the town. Aware we might have to evacuate with little notice, we had packed go-kits for ourselves, stocking our cars with bottled water, no-cook food, changes of clothing and anti-anxiety medication. Delia and Gary and I had formulated our family meeting plan, mapping routes to a village on the other side of the river, upwind of where fallout might fly.

Now it's a year later and suddenly we're scared again: snipers are roaming the area. Within easy reach of our daily doings, 13 people have been shot, ten fatally. We drive on fumes, reluctant to provide a motionless target at a gas pump. We do not do errands; we don't want to visit people if it means going by car. But one Saturday morning, we decide we must go to the big box hardware store—I can't remember for what, but it must have been critical. The store is in a strip mall exactly like those where several of these shootings have occurred. I park the car as close to the store entrance as we can get. I tell Gary to stay put—and, to my great surprise, he agrees.

And then I run. I run like hell. I do not run in a straight line. I zig four steps and then I zag six steps. Everyone else is doing the same thing and I don't even feel silly. When I have secured whatever it was we thought we needed—a bolt, probably, or a gasket—I zigzag back to the car. I'm unharmed. It's amazing, the whole thing. Malvo and Muhammed: complete strangers, unfathomable, invisible and the most powerful people in our lives.

As Winter Comes, 2016

I try for May beneath
the Beech, three children
gamboling, Spring—
loaded, whispering conspiracy
and thrilled inside
the daylong dusk, half-hidden
from the one who seeks,

or for July, one poet, shaded,
watching how the river
runs and rumples, thinking
how to write of it
when both her hands
are unfamiliar,
mottled with striae of sun
as wind disturbs the canopy,

for Labor Day's ironic interval,
tables set for gathering,
the cool trapped
wide and soft below the limbs
still woven shut.

But here's November's tree
laid bare, its openwork exposed
so afternoon falls clear
through netted branches,
lighting snow
though absent any warmth.

December Light

comes low into the room,
falls soft mid-afternoon
around my reading chair
and on my nape
like poultice for
an incidental pain.
Its porous weight
encloses what remains
of shape
when borders disappear.
It is the opposite of words.

I let it fill the master suite,
even the place
where the master would be
if he were home.
But no one's here
so I take off my clothes
and swim, sidestroking
through the lemon air
inside the ease
that wordlessness provides.

Under the Feeder, the Cat

Under the feeder, the cat
accepts the afternoon,
just warm enough
inside a slant of winter sun
to wait an hour
near the barren place
where scattered seed
has killed both weed and grass.

Over her head,
the chickadee is urgent
in its chirruped warnings
to a dove below
that cats outside are never full asleep.

But I agree
that when the feed is plentiful
and cold awaits the first small failure
of the light, the most compelling voice
says eat.

Five Quatrains and Change

Once when we were young

we found a street café we liked
and sat to watch a skillful mime
play mirror to our characters,
a pair of nouns who'd never rhyme

in body or in mind. The view
moved by. A lovely woman stepped
across my sight to lean to you.
Her one eye winked, the other wept.

She raised a hand, erased the wink.
I laughed, you said you had to split
and time ran out the sudden rip.
I hastened toward the Saybrook spit

where shoreline roadways crossed themselves,
intoned your lesser sins and prayed.
I set them straight; I knew, by God,
that you had never deeply strayed.

I raced behind your minute moves
to where the languid seatongues sip
with unabating appetite
at land's receding lip.

I gave the waves my callused feet.
You kissed them from the underneath.

I knew you by your tongue.

Imagining the Unimaginable

Alone inside my room
with baby Delia on my mind,
I try to slip into the moment
at the border
when he wrings her
from my arms, turns her
from the sight of me,
the sound of her astonishment
half-strangled by his certainty.
I pretend the theft,
the halving of myself.
I try to learn the disbelief,
my hands bewildered
at my sides.

I pretend the songs between us –
one for this morning's wakening,
another for tonight --
falling silly on the sand,
try to feel how memory
of her body on my chest,
fragrance of her head
beneath my chin, opening
and closing of her hands
against my neck
escapes.

I pretend her in his careless care
and she not even grown
beyond my carrying, my breasts,
my recognizing how a pain

can pucker on her forehead,
disappear.

I close my eyes to see if I can learn
the awful distance
of a thousand feet, the flat forever
of the desert floor.

I try to feel our illnesses,
mine the understanding nothing,
his the knowing all,
the hollow in us both.
I try to learn the knowing now
how hatred loves a hollowing.

I can't, though, follow learning
to the end. Only in a nightmare
do I feel it all and even there
I struggle up from sleep
unwilling to be left.

Killed

November, 2017

I used to grasp this *killed*. But now I don't.
Baptist prayers hushed, the spirit chilled.
I would have felt this cruelly. Now I can't.

I grieved the suicide of boys so spent
they might as well have died in Afghan hills.
I grasped them killed again. But now I don't.

I took it in, what small draped bodies meant,
the hope and heartbeat of a town gone still.
I would have felt this cruelly. Now I can't.

Warm oceans filled with flotsam, babies sent
to sea to flee a tyrant's murderous will.
I grasped them killed each way. But now I don't.

It didn't help the lost, my small lament,
but I knew grief for every one until
the cruelty was numbing, and I can't.

A sepulcher inside me shut. I'm slant,
deflect the dead, the coffer overfilled.
I used to grasp them killed but now I don't.
I used to feel them cruelly. Now I can't.

Sinkholes

In the middle of an hour
behaving well, a sinkhole
opens under me. It wasn't
then it is. It is the sorry
sibling of the startling joy
of mornings when the cat
does sidestrokes through
the flood of sunshine on the floor
and there is quiet just enough.

My undermind, it seems,
is racketing around some store
of not quite sensibility,
happens on what might develop
shape as someone gone,
an hour of laughter irretrievable,
the painless pervious bones
that hold me up, my daughter grown
and pulling out from underneath
my self's hypothesis.
The shapelessness is only deep.

So good it's never more than blinks
before I snag a handhold
at the swallet's lip. Sometimes it's you,
sometimes the book awaiting me,
the prospect of a change
in furnishings, the table here,
the footstool maybe there,
improving everything.
A conversation in the other room

can make a woven, sturdy bridge.
Or I can simply balance
on the edge until the sinkhole
puckers, disappears.
I have not yet studied how to fall
toward what I can't describe.

The Atheist's Dilemma: Within

I've tried, even prayed
to believe. There came

no enveloping warmth,
no slamming light.

Only the soft smother
of nothing at all.

But there was the whorl
of silk at baby Delia's nape.

There is a diminished
seventh chord,

the minute in December
when day begins its half-year stretch.

There's the red gauze
at the tops of early April trees,

the sleeves of sleep that lift
to fold from underneath,

my husband's fingers tendering
my wrong-way curl, around, around.

My child, a length of light, the drift
from consciousness and music in my hair.

There may be of god in these.

The Atheist's Dilemma: Without

As the April valley slides
between motheaten hills
toward the town below,
it cups a firmament that seems
to rise as the meadow drops.

I cannot see with my usual eyes
this distance of air
and the land belittled beneath.
There's too much sky to understand.
It beggars disbelief.

Even the crooked denuded pine
alone on an outcrop of rock
might be reaching a quill-dry tip
to fasten heaven to earth.

Because the Rain

has blurred the hills across the cove
and turned my neighbor's rutted lawn
into an archipelago

and sky is bundled up in cloud,
light entrapped inside
so lamps come on too early in the day

and all the rooms are sad, windows
barely signified, chairs and beds
diminished in the grey,

I dare not write as I intended
of a friend I loved
who left just short of half my life ago

although I feel her suddenly today,
the good of her, the gone of her,
because the rain.

IV. LITTLE DELIA

The Odyssey: The Short Part of a Long Story

My whole post-college existence could be characterized as a wandering, I suppose. I've lived in a silly number of places, bought and sold a ridiculous number of houses, tacked back and forth across several career paths and marriages. Like Odysseus, I followed strokes of luck and impulse through wonderful adventures, fetching up one place or another and then embarking again for foreign parts. Like Odysseus, though, I had a singular destination throughout. Mine was motherhood. I never doubted my child would, above all other things, make sense of my life.

And so it would be.

During December of 1982, I was so pregnant that I inspired something like panic in the men we trained at FEMA's Emergency Management Institute. Finally, I gave in to my boss's plea to await Delia's birth at home. After five days off, however, I was sick of languor. On the 22nd, I cleaned, arranged shower gifts in the nursery, walked four miles.

As we prepared for bed, my water broke. It broke with considerably more, well, water than we'd been led to expect, but we proceeded deliberately to put house and suitcase in order, mustered stepsons Lee and Chris to manage the bulletin process and set out for the hospital calmly, unaware that all that breaking water was the effect of an abruption, a separating of the placenta from the uterine wall.

We were admitted to the maternity ward, not quite in time to get a bed in a room. I lay on a gurney at the dark end of a hall, invisible in the stir of overbusy maternity staff but perfectly happy, virtually without pain. There was just this question I felt compelled to ask: wasn't I supposed to have a fetal monitor, as they'd recommended in my pre-natal classes? Oh, they said, there was just the one and it was in use. So I simply waited for the real cramps to begin.

Around 1:45, a sweet-faced nurse brought me the monitor, laid it across my belly, watched for a moment and rushed off, muttering, "Oh, my God." Within a minute, my gurney was on the move toward the OR, flanked by my obstetrician, a pediatrician and an anesthesiologist batting about the terrible term "fetal distress". I was headed pell-mell for a Caesarean section, the latest in a series these three had already performed that evening. The anesthesiologist, anticipating the insertion of the epidural needle between my vertebrae, asked me how much weight I'd gained during pregnancy. When I told him thirty pounds, he erupted. "Goddammit, Mayo," he bellowed, "you do this to me every time!" The beleaguered obstetrician merely blew out his breath.

As it happened, I hadn't packed on enough fat to complicate his work. The anesthesiologist was so apologetic that I didn't want to bother him with the news that a past epidural hadn't worked on me. It still didn't: as the C-section began, I could feel clearly the cold burn of the scalpel across my abdomen. Thinking this was be expected, I was silent until the cut went deeper. "Oh, dear," I said.

My new friend, the abashed anesthesiologist, heard me. "Okay," he said, "we'll have you better in one second." And in one second, I was asleep.

I wakened in a private dark, a nurse nudging me gently with news of a hungry baby. My husband stood with his arms full of child. Maybe I'd traveled as the "elderly primagravida" the sign on my bed insisted, but I'd reached home: motherhood.

It was the best odyssey of my life, except for the ones which made up Delia's babyhood, toddler, tween, teen and young adult years and continue until the very minute I type this final period, right here.

Woman Pain

began of course
as she uncoiled
her spacious self

inside that definite
hard bone
splintering

with the thrust
through its own
narrow curve

of wide woman
hips, important
emptiness

where the world
will sleep swollen
and restless

pushing toward
its opening
from her

one anguish
at a time.

The Beginning: Beginning the End

Beginning

As you unfurled and gave me
breadth and rhythm in myself
my happiness drew in to warmth
where you and I conjoined.
You circled blindly
in the space you made of me,
grew me out into the world
while keeping secret
all the songs we shared,
the rippling of a dual life.

End

You were lifted
from our common sleep.
The slow and mutual loss began
and life outside of me
conformed to you, took you
into itself, warmed and lightened
by your primal exhalation,
infant kiss of air.

The Beginning: Alone Without Words for the Loneliness

for Delia

You had no words for the end of your first warm dream,
the scalpel making its perfect savage cut
in the wrap of your blood-dark cocoon,

the hammer of language and cold, the inescapable light
and shock of air in your wakened lungs, your sudden unfolding
in strangers' rude gloved hands and the loss

of the music and rhythm of being inside. You had no words
and all I could offer was my self and wonder
at how surely you moved, so recently crossed from sleep,

to the blessings of breast and touch and song.
You've opened out of so many dreams since then, silent
and stunned at the entry into the next unsuspected place

but somewhere back of thought and word you know the way
to breathe the colder air, inhabit the bigger space
and nourish yourself in the hard prismatic world.

Beyond: The Spirit Regrets

The soul transpiring may flow at the instant of death
into clear, beneficent light or add itself as a whisper
of weight to swift and total night. I pray to reduce into dark.

I would not hover sentient above, my child in the world below.
If the body bereft has the quiet that ever will be, the spirit
must harbor all feeling that ever there was.

What if my child is there alone? My helpless wakeful soul
would hurl itself against the filmy end of light
and whatever remains of the heart would break.

Beyond: Shadow Woman Wants to Say Goodnight

Just beyond the ill-kempt hedgerow bristling
on the borderline of death a little crowd of shades
moves restless, muttering. One is the woman

who died at night, left a child alone to fear
the slide from waking into sleep, the cleavage
of the next day's light. Hers are the hands

that stretch across the bramble wall to lift
the child from her bed for holding again
against the dark. Hers are the hungry fingers

she must snatch back empty just in time.
She plaits them tight across her mouth
to staunch the grief before it slips as keening
into nightmare on the other side.

Hairsbreadth

You test your transit on stuttering feet,
holding me by the eyes,
your hands outstretched toward mine.
You're crowing victory. But this
is the end of your safety in me.

It's those feet that will move you
into the wilding world
toward ruthless fifth grade girls,
cafés with omelets undercooked,
darkened streets and passenger seats.

It's those eyes where every day
we meet, exchanging news,
the eyes I know could empty,
messages erased,
retracted to a nether place.

It's those hands, the delicate play
of tiny bones a bird could break,
and the place betrayed by your pulse
where you could be opened,
languidly set loose from me.

And all I have half a rug away
is the happiness you look into me,
the way your fingers on my face
will tell of love
a hairsbreadth from catastrophe.

Milestones in the Mouth

There's no denying how good it was to close the checkbook on the last visit to our daughter's orthodontist. Why, then, did I feel a tightening of my throat as Delia gave us her first unwired smile? I think this is the answer: by this transformation, Delia had changed from cute kid to lovely girl, soon, certainly, to become beautiful woman. The occasion was bittersweet. Now I see that her teeth marked other important junctures in her growing up.

I loved the toothless phase. That first half-year of rubbery pink smiles involved staggering fatigue, of course, but provided me unadulterated contentment with my place in the world. When I was nursing Delia, I was earning my way, no matter what else I was not accomplishing. I couldn't fold the wash or run out for eggs, but I was utterly, blissfully useful.

The signal that this lovely interdependence was ending was the emergence of her first tooth: she was on the way to being able to nourish herself all on her own. But I loved that little tooth, the Lilliputian toothbrush that sent spit tailing down the front slope of the sink. When, first in and first out, it loosened and left, I was shocked: too soon. Our photo album provides proof that nothing pleased our camera more than Delia's gap-toothed smile. And her lisp softened even her most irritable complaints. Still: too soon.

It's a different kind of cute when the first adult tooth comes in, too big for the face and providing that faint cast of goofiness seen in all third grade school pictures. I didn't mind the hint of the comical in the angling of her front teeth slightly away from each other and somewhat forward of plumb. But the dentist insisted on discipline. In time I grew fond of the silver look that embroidered every laugh and reflected light in slivers and shards. And then the wires came off, her smile became uncomplicated, and another time of becoming ended.

Nothing in my adult life has promoted such instant regression as the insertion of something sharp (or round and buzzing) into my mouth. I certainly don't wish Delia any major dentistry. She should keep flossing, no question. But I'd sit right next to her in any dentist's chair if she needed her mother. She has only to ask.

Onset

My stepson disappeared
while we were arguing,
he at the windowed end
of a long thin room
and I in the shadow
he made. I'd hooked
a new accusation
to the whipping end
of an old complaint.

It was going to hurt
but just as it reached him
he startled and smiled
at the wall. Something there
lit interest in his eyes
and he tilted his head,
intelligent, intent.
He listened to nothing
I could hear. The anguish
we'd made was gone.
He was happy inside

a mime's transparent box.
I tried to breach
its sequestering walls
with salvos, thrusts
of small shrill knives.
I tried to lure him out
with wheedling bits
of honey talk

but I couldn't reach him
whatever I said.

At last his silence
silenced me. Whoever
he was there with
wasn't I and finally I
was not there too.

Blue Fire

After he molested her, my toddler's
teenaged brother broke in two.
She closed herself entire.

She scorned the doctors' figurines
and crayon books with pictures
showing touching, good and bad.

She'd told us all she would, dry-eyed
and in the odd and only way she could:
Remember yesterday

when he was pulling down my pants?
Remember when he took me to the couch?
Remember when he said he was a lollipop?

And that was all we knew till once,
some months beyond that yesterday,
she fled from sleep, careered from room to room.

My hands are wrong, she wailed. *I feel*
a brick in this one and a hair in this.
And then she touched herself and said

in whispering, *I feel blue fire here.*
I held her and she fanned her fingers,
let their burdens fall.

Two decades on, she wept at last
inside her best friend's arms. She told me so.
She'd wept at last. My own blue fire went out.

Calling Names

When first I used his name
to speak of the thing
he had done
I scooped it so hard
from my hatred
it cracked. Now
it leaks fire,
dark and sourness
in my mouth.

If I say it again to him
I want for the hard sound
to hurt him, the soft
to insinuate into his ear
and poison where it
coils and strikes.

I want him to know
how he festers in me
with love turned sick.
I want him to hear
what he changed.

And after I tell him,
I want him whose name
my toddler whispered
from inside my arms,
who touched her,
cajoled with his boy-slick
tongue, divided her childhood
at before, I want him
to fall into silence for me.

There Will Be Pain

for Chris

It isn't the end of the world, they say,
the one we'll continue to rent,
but there will be no having back
the worlds in which he lived.

The one where he, my almost son,
grew slowly out of deepsweet boy,
watched life alert to trouble coming on,
took loving in as if he starved.

And he said this:
If I'd been asked I'd be a bird.

The world he hid, his own
where he could disappear,
return from half
bewildered, half himself.

And he said this:
Miss Nancy, when I meditate I'm nowhere near.

The one he fell from when he
turned us upside down
and, falling, carried Delia too.
We grabbed for her and let him cartwheel out.

And he said this:
The voices told me if I needed to I should.

We only guess the world he landed in,
kaleidoscopic, myriad as infinite,
mapped only by the hand of God
with Chris His Jesus Christ.

And now, so late, he's back in ours
and we in his, a semi-private
nearly nether world, his last,
the doctors say as if he couldn't hear.

And he says this:
There will be pain and then I'm gone.
I have oncology.

We live inside his hours with him,
say little of the grief for all the years
we chose the other child.
He ponders why we're good to him.

And he says this:
Oh, women are so simple.
You love me, I suppose.

I ask if he can take that in,
love's late return.
He gives me lunacy
or poetry.

It is a sheet, he says, *pulled tight across the bed.*

Children's Chorus

The chapel is full of waiting
when the children come like solemn penitents,
each one an emptiness for song.

From either side they come to join before the altar
silent and condensed as soldiers in their uniform
red sweaters, turn to face us, backs to God.

They lift their single voice to find the music,
draw it cool and slender from the heaviness
of air above in church. We're avid,

taking breath to draw it in, its cleansing
knife-edge, grace, disquiet, all.
We like to feel the music enter us and runnel out.

But when they give us the last protracted note,
a shimmer as restless as birds, we send back
sound of something close to pain.

The children are unmoved, spent familiars
of the harmonies we cannot hear,
each one an emptiness of song.

Little Delia: Three Short Novels and an Epilogue

By the time Gary bought outdoor lights to decorate our holly bush, only two strands remained at the hardware store. We've done our best, but the result is that the top of the bush blinks on and off while the bottom burns steadily. Delia confesses that, eying her boyfriend's Crate and Barrel-qualified Christmas tree and the enviable symmetry of his blue and white-lit doorway, she has said, " My family is so whacked out!" I wonder how she feels about being part of a whacked-out family? "Oh," she says, "I love it."

****

Delia is on medical leave from college: she was a first week Freshman on 9/11 when the plane hit the Pentagon, knew we worked nearby and didn't hear from us for all the hours the phone lines were unavailable. Those hours put paid to her willingness to live that far away from us. Now she's working retail at a suburban mall.

It's a Saturday, 5:00 AM and cold. Despite my husband's ministrations, our elderly second car has given up the ghost and I have to get Delia to her pre-sale shift. I'm wearing my purple nightgown, kneesocks that stop at mid-calf after too many hot-water washings, tangerine wool sweater, my parka, ski cap and slippers. Beautiful Delia, stylish even at this hour, laughs and hugs me, says: "Mom, you look so homeless!" But where other than home could such a thing be said?

****

Delia is playing a supporting role in *Man of La Mancha* at the Coastal South Carolina Center for the Arts. We have lunched on her vegan fare (it's incredible how many unhealthy foods soy can imitate) and have watched the cast play afternoon beach volleyball where Delia's talent involves sending the ball on long high trajectories mostly to the left and right of the net. Or backwards. Now we sit in the darkened theater as the show begins, slowly, subtly, in a darkened prison set. Several pitiful creatures, Delia among them, begin to move onstage, acting silent bits of misery. But this is interrupted by the clamorous cheer of a large group of late arrivals, chatting as they try to figure out where their seats are. The rest of us stir in unease until an actor who should enter much later as the resident madman reels suddenly to center stage and, in a brilliant theatrical ad lib, shrieks. Twice. Silence falls. The madman exits. The play moves on.

****

As Delia has.

Afterlife

The phone is mute,
her curfew past.
She always calls.

We face each other
in the living room,
envisioning.

We see the gloss of frozen mist
across a curving rise of road
before the bridge,

her car in spin,
upending
down the gully wall.

We hear the metal casket
groaning as it slips
a final foot

into the creek
where boulders chop
the flow to froth.

That moment is the last
we have of her
from ten o'clock till two

when she comes in
unharmed, abashed,
and somehow not as real

as what we'd learned
about the hours and hours
of years without her

rolling pale and pitiless
through lives we knew
we wouldn't travel fast enough.

Never Quite

At seventeen, my child
was like the dusk,
never quite the light before,
the night beyond.
Becoming, unbecoming,
she was never what she'd been
when last she'd looked
or would be when she woke.
She knew herself as movement
increment by increment
away and toward,
never quite located in herself.
Sometimes she longed
for equipoise, to pause
as equinox, the neap.
But even wishing
threw the balance off.

I tried to hold myself
in her tableau
as still as certainty,
followed her only
with my eyes
as lucent girl and layered woman
raveled and unraveled, both.

To My Daughter, a Woman

I remember noons
when I located
by the shape of
you at end of day.
I remember the seasons
sweet on your skin
when you held me hello,
your body young and strong
and all I wished to gather
and be gathered by.

I remember parsing
every detail of your mood,
angling for your smile,
watching for surprise
to light your face
before you laughed.

I felt we were continuous
in times of pure content.

I am not ready for you
fugitive, the way
you fade from me when I
begin to press. I'm crippled
by the film that falls
between us now,
the untold news of days
we occupy apart.
I never thought you'd live
so far behind your eyes.

If a poem can hold
what suffers
between words,
let this one bound
the loss, the difference
between the you in me
and you a secret
in your own opacity.

Of Delia in Little Boxes

Packing up, I find again the artifacts
saved everywhere, odd hard bits

of molded clay she proffered in memoriam
for newts and fish and cats who died,

pages laddered with her signature, outsized
letters exclaiming her newfound self,

crayoned houses dwarfed by bald emphatic
macrocephali. I tuck them in with other solaces,

even the fossil steadily shedding dust,
the broken Star of David made of sticks.

I cannot throw a thing away:
the minutes hurtle, taking her along

and I am left in what she's made of me,
a bigger place the more for emptiness.

This Is Not That Poem

That poem rockets upward
now and then,
races the entropic stars
until it tires
and I can suck it back into
the sea of its delivery.

This is not that poem.
That poem can also pussyfoot,
brush my grasp
with syllables so soft
I cannot feel them
till they bite
with hypodermic pique.

The body of that poem
is built on Escher's steps,
the poet climbing stanzas
to an up refracted down
and pitching into water
I can't see
until I'm in it looking up.

But this is not that poem.
That poem surrenders Delia,
whose birth was also mine,
now born again in someone else,
another woman's fastening.

V. RECORDINGS

How Poetry Keeps Us from Drowning

We are weavers of the water
parting tendrils of sea grass
in the tides behind our eyes
to see if opalescence
flares in furrowed pools

winding our fingers
with the mottled filaments,
touching them with our tongues
to taste the briny surprise
of what we've been

weaving to find
the colors of intention
layered beneath
the sly cross-hatching
flux of day and night,
the flat similitude of sky.

In Case of Grief

the Poets will take you at night
to the place behind your house
where neighborhood recedes,

trail their fingers in the shallow pond
to make the koi recoil and fret
beneath the ruffling of their moon.

They'll lead you through the careful scatter
of exotic shrubs and annuals
to darker reaches of the yard

where thistle splays. They'll siphon
chill from underneath the hedge,
pour it on your wakened neck

and then they'll nudge you
near the China rose
and numb you with perfume.

They'll help you to recalculate
the fraught and silent distance to the house
where someone turned the lamps off,

climbed the stairs,
her shadow deepening
as she neared the top.

The Artist Errs

What if Georgia misunderstands
a pleasant stir inside herself,
draws the photographer in

to something close to beauty
in the curving lines
of hipbones interposed?

And what if afterward
she feels the moment disappear
and weeps

for making only love
out of the need to lose
the careful mind, to find

the place where trembling starts,
call forth what lies below
the skin of things at rest:

barns that breathe a stillness
men have died in,
sky a gravity suspended,

flowers of a weight and depth
implied in all that women
do not say aloud?

The Writer's Wife: I Report

I lived with a writer long
enough for him to end
one story, pretty good,
about a man who pulls
a turnip from a moat
or maybe his reflection
from a furrowed field.

His stories, faceted
and angular, refracted
light. When morning fell
on what he left unfinished
on the desk, sundogs
scattered on the floor,
blue and green or violet.
They pulsed there
iridescent, shifting shapes
and sliding through me
when I knelt to touch.
Only he could call them back
to gleam inside his plot
almost occult but true.

He sent the finished story off
and wandered void
from room to room.
He'd sewn the secrets in
and they were gone.
No matter how I loved,
he wouldn't feel like much
with them away.

The Writer's Wife: Eve Supports

Not far from Eden's boundary
Eve listens as the world's
first poet versifies
inside the world's first hut.
He rhymes their clothing
on and off. He rhythms
everything he knows
in trochees: *starlight, serpent,*
apples, sinful, fig leaf.
But he chokes on dispossession
at a sonnet's turn.
A stricken man, he falls upon
their viny bed and weeps.

She knows she's guilty
of his insufficiency,
slides urgent fingers
up the shudder of his ribs
to find the cavity
that clever frugal god had made.
She slips her gift for song
into the opening, gives back
the part of him she is.

Restored, he spins
ten stanzas worth of lines
in sequences of iambs,
dactyls, anapests and finally
the sweet spondee
amen. He stops.

One gentle finger on his mouth,
she suffocates a pending poem
so they can revel
in the tiny freighted pause,
so like the one that just precedes
the murmur of applause
when someone at an open mic
declaims the final couplet
of a brisk or baffling poem.

The Art of Thought

Born upstream from where a man immortalizes green
along the riverbank,
a passing thought is idling among rocks
where turtles bask in what is left of August's heat.
It hears the whispers of the painter's stick
and slides from warmth into a chilly current
in the summer-shallow creek,
steers across the rip and fetches up
below the oddity of easel balanced on its spindly stilts
and silent painter fixing all that flows away,
that closes up and drops, or tarnishes and dulls.

Excited by the prospect of eternity, the thought
begins to agitate around the painter's feet.
The painter picks it up and drapes it on his brace,
lets afternoon evaporate its noise. When it has stilled,
he blends it in among the river birch
with careful stroking of his thumb.
His chalk creates the quiet he intends
and all that's left inside the woods' captivity
is echoes of a small idea's beating heart.
A bird mistakes the ticking for the start of rain
and flies to underbrush.

Found Poem

I reach with the tip of my pen
to the back of myself
to feel for poems undelivered,
the ones gestating into nightmare,
wordless dreams that tinge
the hours till afternoon.

I reach and find the moon
deformed, insomniac
with one cheek flat
against a strew of stars.
I tease it out, this canted
sleepless moon with half a smile,
and give it to you as it is

a pleasure simpler than perfection
in what might have been
the quiet desolation
of a January sky.

Kisses and Poems

dispatched with
a kind of economy
the talk they occasion
cannot achieve

meaning much more
than they mean to
or less

received when they're good
with a grateful
amazement: how

did the little thing aimed
at the head cause such
rippling otherwhere?

Seeing Without the I

In trying to communicate the pond
you might confess your pleasure in

    the skimmers
    teasing water
    with the tickling
    of their feet

    the steady musing of
    amphibians ambivalent
    about the privacy
    of slime

    the wading bird in love
    with how the surface cringes
    from the entry
    of her hinge-tight leg

    the clustered lily pads
    each flower cupping
    just enough of summer's weight
    to anchor all the rest

but you should say without the I
the quiet pull of mud, the reach
and depth of green.

In Fug and Slurry, Duff

In fug and slurry, duff, I hear
the effs and arrs. A poet's ear
would catch the cabalistic sound
of darkness, say, where someone drowned,
a depth and suck inspiring fear.

If I were deeper I'd be clear
about obscurity, the sheer
delight of certainty unwound
in fug and slurry, duff.

But as for me, I love the mere
peculiarity, the weird
gymnastics as my tongue moves round
the shape of dead things that abound
inside the stuff gone soft and queer
in fug and slurry, duff.

Six Easy Rules for the Study of Poetry

One

Take the poem that seems the least
like you, that speaks with a voice
you can't exactly place
in a language you know
your grandmother spoke before
its strangeness silenced her.

Two

Go gently into its mouth.
Try to retrieve the shadowy echoes
that murmur away from your entry
and threaten to disappear.
Go with the swallowing.

Three

If you scrape at ideas growing there,
take freely only of seeds.
Don't blow on anything.

Four

Be open to warmth that curls from chill,
to chill becoming sound.

Five:

Descend to the cavern below its heart.
Here are the tides absorbing light.
Be wary of wanting to see yourself
in the pool where others have drowned.
Here is the poet: leave her alone.
She is the irritant making a pearl.

Six:

Depart the poem carefully:
the way out may widen or deepen fast
or narrow until it's too tight.
It's worked of fragile costly stuff
by one who may have learned to hide
but can't subdue the need to signify.

A Love Poem Unabashed

I've never written one.
They're not encouraged
in the circles where I circulate.
If love one must, find metaphors.

But I'm permitted just this once
by my advancing age
to say I love you in a poem.
So here: I love you, little bit
of waterside I see from where I sit.
The air and walk are gentle there
but in the woods five hundred yards beyond
the footing's rough, exciting
off the path. Granite, thrust
through Earth's thin skin
when island chains ran into us,
stands sharp above the forest floor.

Closer to the beach, where
we have felled the trees
for field or view,
the rocks are weather-smoothed
enough to fit one onto next
to make the mending walls
the poet doubts. I love those walls.

I love the sudden softness
of the shore where time
is never idle and what's left of stone
diminishes with every tide

until one day a wave slips up
and carries back the film of dust
that was a mountaintop.
I love that wave we cannot stop.

Perhaps I go too far to put it
on this page, but here's a postscript
not completely unabashed
for poets in their chairs
who know the ragged edges
of the history we live
and capture notwithstanding
the remaining bits
of wild and odd and good around

or lay a sorrow or a riddle
or a flame so deftly in a line
we others feel it as we know it
partly ours
and love us each
as each is loving back.

Delivery Boy: A Ventriloquy

My father
drives for Canada Dry,
me in the cab on Saturdays,
warm in my anorak, tucked
in the corner of door and seat
so I can see both out and in.
In the truck, he is right
where I want him.

At home
sometimes his hands get free
of his intent, make carillons
of knives and forks, send gravy
tiding beneath our mats.
He hugs my mother from behind
exactly the moment she lifts
the tasting spoon to her mouth
or swings me so my boots fly off.
A little too big for the house, he breaks
the things my mother loves and talks
when she wants peace. When he
makes a mistake, she looks away
from the shame of him and he
looks away from me.

But in the sanctum
of his truck my father's knotted arms
are tamed, his hands preoccupied.
He bowls our weight down the pike,
looming over slower cars and knifing
into open lanes. He threads us smooth

through the clotted city streets,
salutes the people staring at him,
admiring his height and certainty.
When he turns to me then
his look holds nothing but knowing
what to do and he has forgiven me
what I saw last night
as I have forgiven him his humility.

How My Garden Grows: A Ventriloquy

With silver bells and cockle shells
and pretty maids all in a row.

Plain and vexed with being compared,
I gather my sisters
just before dawn and plant them,
shapely toes down, in a flower bed
gone barren with too much sun.
As they struggle against the drag
of earth and root, I try to explain:
your colors are anguish to me.
I leave them,
maidens fainting
with pointless grace
into the cockles' hearts.

Free from contrast,
I sow the sound of bells
in the dark warmhearted soil
at the garden's shaded end.
This evening when the breeze unwinds
there will be music for my mother's ear,
as silver and sweet as I can be
and chiming solitude and rue.

From the Wife of the Astronomer Who Discovered Jupiter's Fourteenth Moon: A Ventriloquy

Something luminous
and secretive waits
in the nighttime sky.
My husband, covert
in a spiral of star,
finds her with his
prurient lens. He
will name her now
and so she will be his.

To me he brings
cold hands down
from the cyclopean attic.
They're trembling as he
comes into our bed
but he is only here
to sleep. The rest he has aloft:
discovery of fold and fissure,
mound and dimple, pleasure
that belies his diffidence.

He will not know the way
I fear the sky, violent
with randomness and full
of frigid light, the way
I feel about the moon
who draws him to the hope
of heat around her radiance
and then beds cold in dawn's pale sky,
morning's concubine.

Miss Muffet, the Aftermath:
A Ventriloquy

I'm so ashamed: my flower patch
is slack, the zinnias
complaining of their thirst
and waiting for me with
the simple faith of blooms.
I keep my boots at ready
in the hall; my watering can
is filled. But I am helpless
to confront the yard,
its tuffets and the wildlife there.

My cottage is a clean,
well-lighted place but even so
I twirl my duster anywhere
a gossamer might grow –
beneath the bed,
along the window sash and up
where wall and ceiling meet.

My only visitors are dreams
in which Boy Blue
abandons his sheep
to soothe my shoulder
where I think a feathered feeler
might have brushed.

I sleep to dream
and wake with hope
today I'll brave

the doorway to a world
where spiders teeter
and drop with stealthy grace
from horizontals everywhere.

The Forest Ranger: A Ventriloquy

I climb the shivering stair to scan my beat
in search of a surprise of color,
any sound or smell that isn't mine.

I stare across the furred green hills, swivel
dervishly till birch and hemlock blend
in waves retreating motionless.

My boredom dazzles me. I find
I want to answer all the questions
posed by whippoorwills regardless

of their worth, to carve a tree's initials
on my trunk, rip silence with an aria.
My loneliness has lost nobility.

I'd thrill to watch a raptor arrow
through the bristling surface of the trees,
welcome any agitation in the woods,

even panic of a bird I love, shrill
of warbler overmatched. When curls of air
come new from north and east

and aspen leaves turn backward on the branch,
I want the storm to boil from clouds
collecting in the bowl above my forest's heart.

I ask that fire lance down to strike at trees
drunk dry by gypsy moth, my jimjams stilled
by sear and clangor of the breaking air.

"It's Been Tolled Before": A Ventriloquy

From how the preacher talks, I know
this room is near enough to hell
as I will want to get in this life or beyond.
The fire is nearly screaming
as the bellows urge and urge
and in the cauldron even metal boils,
the slag afloat on pools of bronze.
But for the blaze, there's little light.
Men, their faces caked in char,
disappear in dark.

The boss says this bell's mine. It's me
who knows which tone must be
and writes the measures of the molds
for workers sweating black
while clay and metal pulley up and down,
groaning like the end of days.
It's me who guides their pour
and watches careful day to day
as metal cools and hardens
into readiness to sing.
It's me who says when they can
break out the bell, chisel off the clay.
I polish last when they have filed
the rough spots off.
It's me who sets the writing in.

I send the others home. I want to be alone
when first this church bell chimes.
Alone I work the lathe that shaves
the bell inside to loose the perfect note.

Alone I tap it with a well-turned bar,
rest my ear against it as the clangor dies,
setting down my tools when I am sure
it's God's own music they will hear
from where the sky and steeple meet
and even Preacher's words don't go.

Toto's Say: A Ventriloquy

If I'd wanted to go back
home, I'd have leapt unbidden
through shining green air
and into the widemouthed
basket beneath the balloon

(because I know baskets
especially the ones
with slaplock lids that trap the air
trapped inside you inside

and this was a good one
open and ready to move
on curls of wind already
winding around the ropes
and sliding under its
tentative weight on hard
green ground)

but I wanted to stay
where a dog himself
can sniff out the source of sorcery,
the imagery where magic is,
the end and beginning of dream,

can dream and declaim
the yark yark yark
of things that glisten
and soar against
the wide green carapace
of sky.

The Thinker: A Seventeen

I. Texas Highway 287 eases up the rise toward Santa Fe through grassland pied with failing shrubs and trees.

II. At the near end of a short inexplicable guardrail sits a slender man in jeans with knife-edge creases, buzz cut turned translucent in the pouring sun.

III. Clouds are cleaner than we've ever seen, anvils reaching high behind the buttes.

IV. Hands on his knees, he gazes steadily into the ditch.

V. Imports from New England's density, we stretch to understand the breadth of things.

VI. The man, immobile, has no car. It's long dry miles to anywhere.

VII. Millennia of wind have painted land the greys and greens we pay high sums to reproduce on bedroom walls.

VIII. He's always been inside the scenery.

IX. Towns one crossroad big are thrown like chicken feed along the route, and not a people anywhere.

X. This man doesn't count.

XI. We're careful to obey the signs that bid we slow to 70 a half mile out of town and then, a few feet on, to 35.

XII. Lonely Xmarts, center town, cant emptily toward rusted pumps.

XIII. This man is thinking of two endings to a story about coming home from war.

XIV. He is praying he will not outlive a wayward child.

XV. He is waiting out the return of the woman who finally left him there after he said he'd rather die than go another mile with her.

XVI. He's dreaming, mostly black and white.

XVII. When a semi passes him, he is momentarily cool, very briefly gone.

The Last Word

As he had asked
they put the poet
to the fire when
it is time and there's
a momentary simmering
in his veins and eyes
the slower abdication
of his bones, finally
a sift of dust and quiet
while the fire eats itself

and then a hiss of movement
in the superheated air,
the hum of lines unwritten
licked by flame to rise
from where they lay
inside a snarl of memory

and this the very last
the poet thought,
a couplet tailing into afterglow:

I didn't guess at this for me,
this strange and silver harmony.

VI.

THE WORLD COMING,
THE WORLD GOING

Sacred Silences

The last cloud of the storm
is borne in tatters to the east.
The steeple stands against
a sky as still and deep
as any soundless promise
I might take to heart.

In the country church below
there is, of course, the quiet
we can't hear, the waiting
of believers for the way
to question what emerges
after nature rakes a place
and leaves a sudden hush.

But all around the church
there is the other silence,
hallowed song
of earthly things arising
from the beating of the rain,
the ringing of a meadow
wild with bloom,
music in its flowering.

It will not last another month,
this garden where
we lose ourselves in worship
without knowing that we do.
Rife with melody—
the harmony of yellows' height

with shafts of purple-blue,
the chimes of red beneath—
it calls us to be tuning
all we are to all it is.
We let ourselves
forget fragility.

The World Coming

The Adirondack meadow drowses
under rising thunderheads,
rolls in gentle swells
to wash against the hills.
But underneath, earth's body agitates.
The distant mountain climbs,
two millimeters more, they say,
by Fall.

I concentrate against the limits
of my mind but I'm not equal
to this minuscule ascent.
I cannot hold a billion years,
imagine wide enough
to circumscribe an ancient sea,
the thrusting up of sharp new hills
the water can't contain.

It isn't possible to grasp
the slow and suffocating
crawl of ice across a continent
to carve this meadow,
scour the peaks, leave kettle holes
that fill to overflow
when steep escarpments
slough their snowpack in the melt,
send infant rivers down
to lick their curves and palisades
into the land.

It's work enough to take this in,

this moment resting on millenia
when now and I suspend
between the elderland
and what is brewing overhead.

The World Going

September brings a zephyr
fiddling idly with your hair
and you don't think about its work
on outcrop, gravestone, jetty,
bone or boulder in the wood.

But that near-whisper of a wind
will skim the merest motes
off perpetuity, carry them
till nightfall stills the air

then drop the dusting
to begin the desert
time will make of everything,
everything we trusted
sand.

Sunflowers

Midsummer, there is little else
that satisfies the eye the way they do
in brilliant rows along the road
or caught mid-garden in the worship
of a pagan god. They've lengthened
past the sedum with its hint of rust,
past daisies crowding out
the smaller blooms in curving beds,
the upper crossbar of the fence,
the ornamental grass.

They claim their place in the open
and warmth of nearly sky,
turn their faces to the sun,
pull against the bracing
of their roots to swivel slowly
till the light descends
below a fringe of cattails
in the marsh.

But August finds them heavy
with the weight of summer
taken hour on hour.
They bow in new humility.

The Naturalist

I. For Randy in her Last World

The bride, unsure
of what is killing her,
allows the nurse to raise her bed
and furl her sheet, reveal
the paradox of satin jacket
with its piping and its ruche
around her chin. Her mouth
is loosened by bewilderment
and when she speaks
the words fall soft and blurred.
She's seeing without aim,
her heavy glasses
set aside for wedding.

The groom is searching
for her gaze,
echoing the minister
much louder than he should,
each syllable a gift, a lie of sorts.
She's hearing that he doubles her,
he understands
he's giving half away.

The ones who love them,
families and keepers
weeping part from happiness,
press around the bed,
repelling time.

II. For David in His Next

Inside the white enclosure
of her room, the wife sleeps
toward the ending
of their life. He's silent,
part of him already part
of where she's gone, so separate
from earth it dizzies him.

But Tuesday when she dies
he'll know to go out
to the autumn marsh,
his thoughts triangular, narrowing
to snakes and bullfrogs
in this world descending
into winter's dormancy.
He'll feel himself complete again,
knowing how to join with cattails
and the stillness of the sky,
not suffering nor meaning harm
when, fingers pinched exactly so,
he lifts the basking Moccasin
to read its message
scrolled against the empty graven air.

Persisting, 2019

I love the winter quiet of my violets,
the way they sleep the sleeping time,
their offering no more than soft
with green beneath.

I hardly mind, of course, their answering
a plenty of the light with summer bloom.
But this year I admire much more
how they persist despite.

I feel that way about a plainsman, staring
at the homestead spun to splinters,
pledging to restore and weeping with a tattered joy
that wife and child survived.

I feel that way about the vigilants
and writers who must pitch themselves
against such infamy
the words they choose may never penetrate.

I feel that way about my self, this body
with its small repairs still muscling me
the ways I want to go.

Most always I am grateful to persist. Except
I find I'm frightened to outlive.

Don't let me outlive the giraffe.

Trespasses

The young retriever tethered
to a campus tree
surveys the traffic eagerly
for any kind of company.
A chipmunk, moving
like a feathered weft
through shafts of light,
strays just inside the radius
of the puppy's rope.

I watch unwilling
as the rope snaps taut,
the chipmunk fixed
beneath an outsized paw,
his tail straight up.
The little dog explores
the frozen creature with its mouth,
nudging, nuzzling, gentle
till it scoops him up.
The jaws close halfway
on a writhe of fur and then,
as if the puppy had to laugh,
they spring apart.

The chipmunk churns
on the lolling tongue,
slides to the grass
over slavered teeth,
propels himself in sine curves
into the underbrush.
I think we've won.

And then he falters,
stops as if to listen
to himself, obeys
a pulling down, surrendering
the stubborn will
that bore a ruined body
from the first bewilderment
into the last.

He wrests three breaths
and cedes the last one
in a sigh, one forepaw tucked,
the other reaching
for the afternoon.

Mothers

We're heading home along the Trolley Trail,
immured in granite here but opening
to cross the marsh before it reaches town.

We squint to clarify an animal ahead,
mid-path and stopped and interested
in us, gaze unwavering.

Anesthetized by spring and sea,
I feel my fear as small and feathery
until her broom-tailed pup appears.

I always dial for answers in emergencies.
The expert in my phone is definite:
do not engage with mothers in the wild.

    When Stephanie performed
    a carpool satire
    of my child, I didn't

    but I could have stopped the van,
    plucked her from the back,
    set her facing me and held her gently

    by the earlobes, said to her:
    You do that thing again
    I'll lock your little face up with a look.

    They didn't but my hands were mad enough
    to pinch until my thumbs
    and fingers met.

As mothers go, coyotes may be more like me
as might have been than was. She trots toward us,
haunches like the pistons in a well-oiled car.

We watch her, rooted. No, he says,
the expert in my phone, don't look at her.
Turn slowly and go back the way you came.

But I am weak against suspense.
I glance behind and see her move aslant
into the woods, grey blur in green.

My expert says we can resume the journey home
when she has gone. Make noise, he says,
when passing where she disappeared.

We cross her track, both clapping wildly
all the while as if she'd been a magic trick.
The tourist coming up the trail from town

is awed by our applause. He stops, backs up,
then turns his tail, retreats. We hear him thinking:
Wildlife. Don't engage.

Getting Glide

A ring-necked pheasant
paces frantic at our yew-lined fence.
His plumage gleams in flickers
as he darts from light to shade
and back. It's sickening,
such terror in a bird whose colors
I can't translate into words.

I call a wistful wildlife
bureaucrat who teaches me:
Connecticut has beaten back
the pheasant's sheltering woods,
cut down its meadow grass.
This bird, he says, belongs
to someone's backyard coop,
captive to our need for beautiful.
And so it is. His owner comes
and gulps him in a net,
then folds him to her chest.
His umber eye rolls wild
and feathers angle off the wings.
He breached his cage, she says,
flew up on unaccustomed wings
and got his glide.

The bureaucrat reminds me
we're in mating time when even this
unearthly bird is urged to blind
researches in the neighborhood,
impelled by a testosterone high.
"Or low," I say, "depending
on your point of view."

Bugs in Love

When I flick the screen
as gently as I can,
the tiny insects coupling
near a ragged hole
spring out into the air.

They whiffle to the deck
still joined, preoccupied,
perhaps, by flight,
or so heroic in their love
they will or can not part.
They land with no more impact
than my farewell word

and after only moments
of confusion between
fore and aft,
they travel twain
into the gap between two boards.
Their babies will be fearless,
I suppose.

Mercy

The flies we couldn't kill last Fall
now lob in lazy spirals toward the light

thick as thumbs, improbable
as zeppelins, dizzying the air with hum.

They're dying now, bumbling
against cold window glass

or burring upside down in shafts of sun,
stirring motes with feeble flourishes,

cradling in their whiskered legs the bulge of air
that carried them before they fell.

Ants

Little by little the flow
of tiny hunter-gatherers
around the kitchen sink
begins to ebb: the traps
work better than we'd hoped.

At first when ants were
multiplying maplines
on our windowsill
and countertops, I grabbed
for anything that sprayed
and doused the forward line,
backing fast away
as if they might fight back.

Instead they tucked their heads
into their narrow waists
and died, but not, I think,
before they bawled
their cataclysmic news
in antish frequencies.
In moments, all their relatives
descended from the hole
above the stove
our builder overlooked.
Like us behind an accident,
they had to witness
what they feared to see.

Today we've scattered
poison cups, a comfort
to the species we are.

The ants are dying now
in privacy. Toxicated colonists
go home—exactly as the wrapper
said they would—to give a pal
a goodbye kiss and so ensure
a heaven full of friends.

The Voice of the Turtle

Something I mistake
for fast food waste
drifts toward us
across the opposite lane.
I slow. This bit of detritus
has feet.

I stop. Gary, sucker
for those without voice,
ejects from the passenger seat.
He flaps a warning
at the baffled drivers
beginning to jam behind.

I flash my lights
at those oncoming
shrieking *No* and *No*
from tight inside
my air-conditioned car.
Good humans all, they brake
and then inch carefully
around the trustful turtle,
all except the Harley man,
leatherbound and helmeted,
who pulls his hog aside,
dismounts, strides
careless of the traffic's press
to pluck the creature
in fat-gloved hands
and slide it gently
back into its pond.

And everyone involved
is gratified except,
perhaps, the turtle
who is thinking, Jesus,
what's a fellow have to do
to get to the other side?

Spider Man

He's handsome in a standard
sort of way, sweet-faced
and young, but God,
he's chosen killing
for his livelihood.
He prowls my porch,
his lethal little spray in hand.
And I encourage him.

Look way up there, I say,
where tiny spiders have begun
to foul my vinyl siding,
webs entrapping not just bugs
but every mote of dust and fluff
this season throws about.
Soon their macramé
of filament and dirt
will cover what I want
pristine.

What taught me this?
Who didn't mention spiders
when the *shalt not kill* went out?
What makes me think
a spider's soul is smaller
than my own?

Once I interviewed a boy
who said he stopped his Elavil
when he went vegan,
said his shadow lifted when

he started looking heifers
in the eye.
I understood, believed.

But now my spider man and I
prepare to liquidate
a hundred creatures, none
more deadly than a jujube
with legs, those legs
less dangerous than hairs
I pull from underneath my chin.

I show him where they are,
whole families whose ghosts
I'm pretty sure will mass
to greet my spider man and me
as we approach
the gates of Hell.

Anansi and I

A nightmare of a spider
with the markings
of an Aztec alien
commands a web
that spans the width
of someone's outdoor fireplace.

He hangs above two MREs,
a tiny sweat bee and a moth,
the latter wholly swathed
in silken burial wrap,
the other struggling,
head and front legs free.

I stop a moment to decide
which animal to serve,
the hungry spider
who has worked all night
to ready lunch
or lunch not going
gently into night.

Positioned back as far
as arms permit,
I work a brittle leaf
to extricate the bee.
Threadwork trembles
and the spider flees
to somewhere I can't see.

The quaking web
is left behind, the bee
now bound by sticky
silver threads to leaf and me.
I'm using an abandoned screw
to pry the insect loose,
my surgery the fireplace shelf,

when suddenly the spider
is advancing on me,
wicked double-jointed legs
jerking fast and high
above his horrid
two-orbed head.
The bee, the leaf and I
take flight, a scream
stuck halfway up my throat.

At noon I find Anansi,
perched again mid-web,
his many legs
unraveling the packaging
around what I had left him
of his midday meal.

VII. THE WHITE-HAIRED WOMAN

The White-Haired Woman Prepares
to Go to Town

She faces herself in the mirror hung
too high above a parlor plant,
checks off the necessaries:
brooch, gloves, good wool suit,
a little powder and rouge.

She starts to turn away and pauses,
gives her reflection a closer look,
dips in her pockets, deepens a furrow
that lowers the brim of her little hat.

Where did I put my smile? she says.
I had it the day the gas man came.
I haven't been anywhere since.

She closes her eyes to think
then fixes herself with a pale blue gaze.

What in Godiva's name have I done with it?
Where in the Helen of Troy is my smile?

She searches her person frantically,
inside a seam, a sleeve, her ear.
Resigned she moves without it
to the door. As always
when she's given up,
the answer comes to her:

I put it in the wash.

She carefully picks up the smile from where
she draped it with her underthings
in the low-lighted laundry room.
She holds it up to her face.
It is very red with lipstick,
illumines the area under her nose,
but, shiver, she says, ah fuck, she says,
it shrank.

The White-Haired Woman Is

though you may overlook her
in buses   luncheonettes
at mass   tucked into chairs
in doctors' waiting rooms
perhaps your eye records her
smaller than she is
perhaps the space she occupies
is not fulfilled

perhaps it is you do not want
to see her as she is
        so much alone
her hemline scallopy
her lipstick cumulating
in the corners of her mouth
the way her milky eyes
betray her expectation
disappointment comes

but you should know
while you are overlooking
her she's watching you
        your flash and churn
the birdlike things you make
of smile and touch
as you maneuver now
        to next

she takes you in
as time ahead absorbs
your days, and hour by hour

you slide toward the circle
of her soft obscurity
the color of her anonymity
the size of caring not so much
for noise

On Obasute Mountain

She conjures the village,
its people enclosing
the little space she'd been,

her skillful sons, silent
daughters, their hands
plunged into the belly

of whale to find
the glister and heat
and coil of viscera—

children she delivered
into a cloud
of rufous steam,

into the damping shock
of frozen air—
now abandoned by her

one more time, mother
pulling back from
tethering

to where she lives
within herself alone
until the hunger

pulls her inside out
and endless winter
sings her heart to sleep.

Waiting Room, ER

It smells of drought, the room where sad small
Sunday troubles queue along the walls. Farther in

behind a soundproof door the truly wounded lie, absorbed
in pain or lassitude they can't remember how to fight

alone. Out here, the lesser miseries await their turn.
An adolescent frowns with migraine, watching glassily

as mayhem moves her back to later in the line.
An ashen woman coughs into her sleeve, succumbs

to the silence her husband creates. A boy is drowsing
in his mother's arms, entrusting himself to her

as he has not for years. My daughter burns beside me,
fingers twitching in her lap.

Suddenly the muffling door swings open with its soft
hydraulic hiss. A voice shouts twice: *Asystole!*

We turn to look around the waiting room as if
to count our group: nobody lost.

Before the door has shut again, we hear a man as he
begins to cry and almost can't, and then his wauling, freed

and terrible, curls us back into ourselves. We're quiet,
listening for heartbeats in the room beyond

where someone rides the seconds steadily away
from daylight and the waiting room, the door.

Diagnosed

As always,
she engages us
with her narrow laughing hands
and small mistakes of dress,
embraces us in curvatures
of voice and smile.
Today, as always,
her approval makes us
better than we are.

But now she says
she's more and less
than what we see.
Invisible at first, a shadow
trails her, half a step
behind.

She lifts her quick voice clear
and we try to follow,
grasp her different
from the dance of her hands,
the charm of her argyles
and red barrette.
But we're reliant
on how large she loves,

though she seems small
inside the weight
of waiting near the dark.

Palpation

It's not my fingers haven't told me
truths about a ripening summer peach,

the underside of leaves
and warmth retained in the evening's lake.

It's not they wouldn't understand
the need to move like whispering

beneath my daughter's hair,
around my husband's mouth.

But when I make them probe
the complex privacy of my breast

invade its unresisting slide
across the mooring of my bones

my fingers are clumsy and reckless,
carnival seers foretelling my chances

of grief, romance, longevity,
declaring tragedy from mere abundance

or hurrying past some grain of truth
too hard to understand.

I'd rather let them gather into comfort
underneath this density of flesh, hold me

in suspense and tell the simpler story
of my weight and heat, passivity.

Rhythm

I see myself one
of a trio of women
lined up on the porch
of a respite in Lyme

soft in our slippers
and quiet as Sunday
dreaming in circles
straight in our chairs

rocking to rhythms
in what is remembered
of sewing and weeding
and stirring the soup

making the floorboards
resound to the cadence
of suckling and soothing
and scolding a child

dancing to music
of teenagers caroling
secrets and promises
into the phone

moving to peace
in the rising and falling
of somebody's breathing
beside us in bed

seesawing over
a faltering heartbeat
back and forth over
a funeral hymn

pressing the curve
of the rocking chair runners
backward on sorrow
forward on death.

In the Long Afternoon of My Life

I idle in the hour when sun
slides down to backlight feathered grasses
in the marsh, turns Jacob's Beach to suede,

pick my way out tumbled rocks
to where the sea divides
along the jetty's prow,

watch the shallow combers press
in quick succession toward the shore,
rise to reach for drier sand and topple short.

They slide beneath the ones behind
to scour where they have been before,
the way I do, my hours awash

with what slips back from yesterday,
just now the vague vibration
of an antique love affair and someone

I have tried to shed who prowls
along the northern edge of memory
while I look south across the Sound.

Nostalgia Praecox: July, 2019

I.

The heralding gold of forsythia
has already gone to green
before I have time
to pay it proper joy.
No matter how many their ranks,
I can't secure in memory
the orange of impudent lilies
along the road.

Even the blousing of peonies
before they begin to bow
reminds me of what it's like
when they're not there.
The scent of the short-lived
lilac belongs, for me, to tragedy.

The more of glorious there is,
the more I rue it coming gone.
I'm trying to memorize
leaves.

II.

The more I always cherish
the lengthening days,
the more I never celebrate
those minutes of dawn and dusk

the solstice brings
and time takes back next day.

III.

The more I love
the clear-eyed women
and men in my circles
of word and work—
the warmth
of someone's shoulder
next to mine—
the more the time we share,
the more I know
the struggle not to try
to temper love before
time's tempering.

Making Wake

I say to you that
when I die I hope
it's I receding not you

and you nod as if
this were good between us
and so I picture

you still vivid,
me on the dreamy fade,
absorbing slowly

into gloaming, smile
inkling in the dark,
my last little quarrel

with traveling alone
no more than riffle
in my wake.

NOTES

P. 7: "Shell Gas Attack." My grandfather, Captain John K. Meneely, Sr., wrote this poem as part of a letter home from a trench in northern France during WW I. This one was prefaced thus: "My first poetic attempt under shell-fire".

P. 80: "The Rhythms Gone Awry." In Northampton Hospital in 1976, women seeking abortions were hospitalized overnight in the part of the ward which housed women suffering problem pregnancies.

P. 163: "It's Been Tolled Before." A silent movie showing work inside the Meneely Bell Foundry in Watervliet, NY, opens with a slide announcing "It's Been Tolled Before." Bell aficionados say that Meneely bells are among the finest in the world and toll in countries around the globe. Locally, Meneely bells hang in steeples in the First Congregational Church of Old Lyme and the Indian Hill Cemetery Chapel in Middletown.

P. 166: "The Thinker: A Seventeen." With a nod to Mark McGuire Schwartz, who invented this poetic form.

P. 179: "Persisting, 2019." As of July, 2019, giraffes are now on the endangered species list.

P. 193: "Anansi and I." Anansi is a beloved spider trickster in West African mythology. MRE is a militaty and disasster response team acronym for *Meal Ready to Eat.*

P. 201: "On Obasute Mountain." The Japanese definition of "obasute" is "abandoning the granny". Women too old to help sustain the community were conducted, preferably by a son, to Obasute Mountain to die in solitude.

P. 208: "Nostalgia Praecox: July, 2019." The *algia* in nostalgia means "pain"; the *nost* means "homecoming". It can be taken to mean "homesickness" and was viewed in the 18th century as a disorder of the brain.

ABOUT THE AUTHOR

Nancy Fitz-Hugh Meneely, Smith College B.A. in hand and nothing at all to suggest she knew how to make a lesson plan, began professional life as an English teacher in Vermont's Waterbury High School. When, after two happy years, Vermont suggested it was important that she sport a real credential, she acquired a Master of Arts in Teaching from Yale. After discovering her best students were listening to her from inside hallucinations, she moved into the work of training community/school teams in drug abuse prevention at Yale's Drug Dependence Institute. Later, with a Master's of Education in Human Relations from the UMass School of Education, she tacked back and forth across a career path in training, counseling, and education, finishing paid employment in a twenty-year career with the Federal Emergency Management Agency in Washington, DC, where she worked first in emergency management training and then directly in support of response and recovery operations. She retired north, where she lives what Baron Wormser calls "the poetry life" on the beautiful Connecticut shoreline, happily engaged in writing, discussing, judging, teaching and performing readings of poetry. Her first book, *Letter from Italy, 1944*, provided the libretto for an oratorio composed by her sister, Sarah Meneely Kyder, performed most recently by The Hartford and Greater Middletown Chorales along with the Hartford Symphony Orchestra at the Bushnell in Hartford. *Letter from Italy, 1944* was named by the *Hartford Courant* one of thirteen important books produced in 2013 by Connecticut writers.

This book is set in Garamond Premier Pro, which had its genesis in 1988 when type-designer Robert Slimbach visited the Plantin-Moretus Museum in Antwerp, Belgium, to study its collection of Claude Garamond's metal punches and typefaces. During the fifteen hundreds, Garamond – a Parisian punch-cutter – produced a refined array of book types that combined an unprecedented degree of balance and elegance, for centuries standing as the pinnacle of beauty and practicality in type-founding. Slimbach has created a new interpretation based on Garamond's designs and on compatible italics cut by Robert Granjon, Garamond's contemporary.

For more information on the work of Nancy Fitz-Hugh Meneely,
please visit www.antrimhousebooks.com/authors.html.
Copies of this book are available at all
bookstores, including Amazon.

CPSIA information can be obtained
at www.ICGtesting.com
Printed in the USA
FSHW020354250220
67495FS